◀◀ THE **A–Z** OF RECORD LABELS ▶▶

Printed and bound in Great Britain by MPG Books Ltd,
Bodmin,Cornwall

Distributed in the US by Publishers Group West

Published by: Sanctuary Publishing Limited, Sanctuary House,
45–53 Sinclair Road, London W14 0NS, United Kingdom

www.sanctuarypublishing.com

Copyright: Brian Southall, 2000. This edition, 2003

Cover design by Ghost

Photographs: Courtesy of Pictorial Press unless otherwise stated.

While the publishers have made every reasonable effort to
trace the copyright owners for any or all of the photographs or
images in this book, there may be some omissions of credits,
for which we apologise.

ISBN: 1-86074-492-3

◀◀ THE **A-Z** OF RECORD LABELS ▶▶

BRIAN SOUTHALL

Sanctuary

BIBLIOGRAPHY / ACKNOWLEDGEMENTS

In addition to information gathered by the author during 30 years of working in the music business, and from interviews carried out for previously issued publications or radio programmes, the author has referred to other published works and gratefully acknowledges the following titles:

Holzman, Jac and Daws, Gavan: *Follow The Music* (First Media Books)
Dannen, Frederic: *Hit Men* (Random House)
Smith, Joe: *Off The Record* (Pan)
Shaw, Arnold: *Honkers And Shouters* (Colier Books)
Wexler, Jerry: *Rhythm And Blues* (Jonathan Cape)
Coleman, Ray: *The Carpenters* (Boxtree)
Gordy, Berry: *To Be Loved* (Headline)
Branson, Richard: *Losing My Virginity* (Virgin Publishing)
Kennedy, Rick and McNutt, *Randy: Little Labels – Big Sounds* (Indiana University Press)
Rust, Brian: *The American Record Label Book* (Arlington House)
Hardy, Phil and Laing, David: *Faber Companion To 20th-Century Popular Music* (Faber & Faber)
Bronson, Fred: *Billboard Book Of Number One Hits* (Billboard)
Rosen, Craig: *Billboard Book Of Number One Albums* (Billboard)
Guinness Book Of Hit Singles and *Guinness Book Of Hit Albums* (Guinness Publishing)
Larkin, Colin: *Virgin Encyclopedia Of Popular Music* (Virgin Publishing)

Thanks also to all of the people employed at record companies, large and small, who agreed to be interviewed and who supplied information, company histories, photographs and company logos. Finally, I would like to thank Iain MacGregor and Chris Harvey at Sanctuary Publishing for determining that there should be a second edition of this book and for their enthusiasm and support to make it a 'better' book.

FOREWORD

BY CHRIS WRIGHT

The role and importance of record labels have changed considerably over the years. In the days of vinyl, labels were easily recognisable and there was often a style and quality of music that one came to expect and associate with each label, for example Motown, Atlantic, Chrysalis, Elektra, Asylum, A&M or Island. Also, the logos of each particular label – such as the Chrysalis butterfly, the A&M trumpet or Island's palm tree – were instantly recognisable. Nowadays, with the concept of CDs, it is often difficult to see the logos of the different record companies, and with artists demanding their own label names and designs it is a sad fact that record labels do not seem to be as important as they once were.

When Terry Ellis and I started out as managers of Jethro Tull, we were not specifically attracted to the idea of starting a record label. However, having failed to secure a viable record deal for the group, we negotiated a production deal for them with Island Records, which meant that, in return for a certain number of Top Ten records, we would have any other records by artists that we produced released on our own label. Hence the start of Chrysalis Records.

Having launched the label successfully, I remember some years later suggesting to A&M, Island and Virgin that we all combine to form one company. Unfortunately none of the principals were interested in such a concept, but I have no doubt that, had such a merger taken place, we would have created a record company that would have changed the face of the music business.

Today, the amounts of money being offered by the majors to new independent labels are very attractive, but strangely the majors don't always understand what makes an independent label successful. It appears that, having spent a considerable amount of money buying the label, acts are dropped, staff are fired and the label's identity becomes lost.

Fortunately, however, there will always be a need for such independents, because they tend to believe in acts in the longer term. For instance, our Echo label has persisted with the band Moloko when a major might have dropped them after their second, slightly disappointing album. It's also interesting to think that, were it not part of the Chrysalis Group, by now the Echo label would probably have been bought up by a major.

Selling the original Chrysalis Records label was a terrible time for me. It was a financial necessity at the time, but it certainly caused me many sleepless nights. Thankfully, I have been able to continue in the music business through Echo, the Hit label and more recently Papillon Records. Looking back now, I can see that labels such as A&M, Atlantic, Island and Motown were the great independents of earlier generations before Chrysalis came along. In those days, labels were an extension of the personalities and, in some cases, the egos of their founding fathers.

Today there are still some brave pioneers around launching their own independent labels alongside the established 'big five' global companies. Long may they all – independent and major – continue to flourish.

CHRIS WRIGHT, chairman of Chrysalis Group plc, a publicly-quoted media, music and entertainment company including the Echo, Hit and Papillon record labels. He launched the original Chrysalis Record label in 1968, created the Chrysalis Group in 1985 and sold the original record label to Thorn EMI in 1991.

INTRODUCTION

Record labels are fascinating things. Not the bits of printed paper which were stuck to the end of early cylinder recordings, nor the first round labels which were attached to the centre of discs as long ago as 1901, but rather the actual companies and labels which were responsible for bringing you and me – and millions of others around the world – the best of recorded music.

The reason why record labels – the bits of paper – came into being was quite simple. Even before the arrival of the 20th century, the need to identify what was on a cylinder or disc, the name of the artist and the company which made the recording, was recognised both in order to establish ownership and also to publicly acknowledge and promote the performer's credentials. As this method of identification established itself throughout the international music industry, so the quality and style of the music on each record gradually came to be associated with particular labels or record companies, and as more and more companies and labels were formed it became clear that many of them were deliberately linked with particular genres of music, from classical to jazz, blues to country and from rock 'n' roll to soul.

This book is about some of those record labels and companies, although not all of them, because there are too many to mention. (A leading British music trade directory carries over 30 pages of record company listings, with over 50 entries on each page, and that just covers the ones operating the UK!)

The 200+ record companies and record labels featured in this book represent some of the oldest and youngest; the thriving and the defunct; the independent and the corporately owned. There are American and British giants alongside smaller European and Asian operations and specialist labels covering all types of music. But there will still be labels I have omitted, which others will claim deserve a mention over some that I have included. Sorry, but someone had to make a choice, and that someone was me.

There are those who argue that record companies and labels are unimportant as far as the record buying public is concerned, that if people like a record then they'll buy it irrespective of the label it's on. While this is undoubtedly true, there was a time when, by virtue of a recording being issued on a certain label, you knew what sort of record or style of music to expect: Okeh's early blues recordings; the first Atlantic releases for great R&B records; Chess records for the best in American 1950s blues; Motown's new style of distinctive soul music; Parlophone's 1960s Merseybeat releases; Elektra's innovative folk and rock music; the Stiff collection of pub rock and punk titles; credible and commercial rap from Def Jam; the best in techno music from Mute; consistently great jazz from Verve; and a hundred years of classical quality from DG.

If the biggest-selling and most popular labels have abandoned that dedication to a particular style of music, it is because, from the '50s onwards, popular music grew to be a big business. Record companies had to accept the fact that people's musical tastes had changed and become more cosmopolitan.

Then the larger record companies decided they could be all things to all men. They signed rock and sought out pop; they linked themselves with overseas labels to obtain local rights to hit records; they experimented with the avant garde and, in many cases, launched subsidiary labels dedicated to underground, punk, disco or dance music in the same way as existing specialist classical or jazz divisions.

All of this – along with stories of the extraordinary, dedicated, sometimes larger-than-life characters who started or ran record labels – is what is fascinating about record companies and record labels: how labels have been launched in obscure towns by people who were record retailers, local DJs, booking agents or artist managers; and how companies were set up in the major cities by club owners, former music business executives, singers and songwriters. While some prospered others went bankrupt, and some survived for only a few years while others continue today under the umbrella of a larger corporation.

Setting up and running a record company is a business. People did it as a job – not necessarily to get rich but certainly never with the idea of becoming poor. There were those who did it for the love of music, the desire to make and then make available to a wider audience something that had excited them. There were others who saw the music business as a good investment, offering a handsome return on their money, and as in so many businesses there were those whose intentions were less honourable, who cheated artists out of their rightful rewards.

Since the emergence of the first record operations over 110 years ago, companies and labels have sprung up in the most extraordinary places and in many cases the registered name gives a clue to the origins of a business. They have been named after countries, states and cities; had titles created from the initials, first names and surnames of their founders; and names formed in honour of buildings, statues and streets.

Anyone with even the remotest interest in music knows the name of a record label. They may not know why they remember it, and they may not even know the names of any of the artists who recorded for the label, but for some good reason it has stuck. Many people of a certain age – in my case over 50 – will recall the Embassy label with affection and fondness, and while it doesn't rate an entry in this book it does have a place in many hearts as the label launched by high-street retailers Woolworths probably in the late 1950s or early 1960s, releasing cover versions of the best-selling hits records of the time. Rumour has it that the likes of Engelbert Humperdinck and Elton John made their first records for Embassy, recording under other names.

So when is a record label a record label? Even though we have listed the total number of US and UK Number One albums and singles for each entry (up until June 2003), the criterion is not how many hit records a label has to its credit: creativity, imagination, vision and achievement are some of the qualifying essentials, along with risk, investment, determination and commitment. Companies launched by individual artists solely as a platform for their own recordings, for financial or any other reason, were not considered to be record labels. There has to have been an investment, both financial and artistic, in artists and repertoire (A&R), and that has come over the years from both the brave and, in some cases, foolhardy individuals who launched their own labels and the large corporations that gave an executive his or her head to create an outlet for new talent.

If all of that began nearly 115 years ago, it's amazing, refreshing and reassuring to know that there are still people around today – and who will be around tomorrow – who will borrow money from their parents, take out an expensive bank loan or impress a friendly investor just so that they can start their own record label. They will follow in the footsteps of many of the great and talented people who created the labels and companies compiled in this book. The music lovers of the world should thank them all.

A

A&M

TRUMPETER/PRODUCER HERB ALPERT AND PRO-
DUCER/PROMOTION MAN JERRY MOSS FOUNDED
THEIR FAMOUS RECORD LABEL IN 1962, and used
the initials from their surnames to create A&M. Continuing
their obsession with initials, when the pair launched a new
label in 1994 they named that one Almo, using the first two
letters from each surname. Alpert initially turned to running
his own record company only after a brief and unsuccessful
singing career with RCA, who actually turned down his sug-
gestion that he should play the trumpet for the label.

In 1966, Alpert and Moss bought Charlie Chaplin's old film
studio in Hollywood and used it as the headquarters for A&M
Records. The label's first success came with Alpert's 'Lonely
Bull', which was followed by releases from The Sandpipers,
Sergio Mendes and Chris Montez. Early A&M releases were
issued in the UK through Pye International until 1967.

Lou Adler had co-managed surf act Jan And Dean with
Alpert until the latter decided that the act's days were
numbered and that he was going to focus on playing the
trumpet. He was later invited to join forces with his former
partner again and link his Ode Records with A&M, which
involved them releasing Carole King's *Tapestry* album.
However, a visit to the Monterey Pop Festival in 1967 left
Moss reflecting on the fact that there wasn't one A&M act on
the bill, and he set about acquiring the US rights for hip acts
such as Cat Stevens, Free and Humble Pie. Leon Russell later
took his Shelter Records into the A&M camp, alongside direct
signings Joe Cocker, The Carpenters, Stealer's Wheel, Rick

No 1
Singles **26**
Albums **15**

No 1
Singles **10**
Albums **14**

A&M

Wakeman and Supertramp, and the label grew to be one of the world's leading independent companies.

The world-famous duo of brother and sister Karen and Richard Carpenter signed to the label in 1969 for an advance of $10,000 and a 7% royalty on records sold, and they went on to sell over 20 million records, while label founder Herb Alpert and his Tijuana Brass topped the 30 million sales mark.

Throughout the '80s, Alpert and Moss maintained their high level of involvement, and multi-million-selling acts such as Squeeze, The Police, Janet Jackson, Bryan Adams and Sting brought A&M to the attention of the major record corporations. Alpert and Moss sold their company to Polygram for a reported $500 million in 1989, but they remained involved with the label until 1994, when they severed their connections before re-emerging with Almo.

While the likes of Sheryl Crow and Dina Carroll continued to earn success for A&M, owners Polygram found themselves the subject of an acquisition by Seagrams Universal Music Group, as a result of which A&M ceased to operate as a separate company. The label became an imprint for artists going through Universal's Interscope division, alongside Geffen, and in 1999 the parent company sold off the Chaplin film lot that had been home to A&M for over 30 years.

No 1
Singles **16**
Albums **3**

No 1
Singles **1**
Albums -

ABC-DUNHILL

FOUNDED IN HOLLYWOOD IN 1955, ABC WAS A SUBSIDIARY OF THE PARAMOUNT PICTURE COMPANY, and entered the music business as a distributor for records released by the Disney company. A number of rock 'n' roll and pop acts appeared on the label, such as Paul Anka (who held the Number One spot in the UK for nine consecutive weeks with 'Diana' when just 15 years of age), George Hamilton IV, Lloyd Price and Danny And The Juniors. Many of these acts were brought to the label via ABC TV's *American Bandstand* show, hosted by Dick Clark, who acted as an adviser to the label.

Moving into black music in the '60s, ABC signed The Tams and The Impressions to the label, adding Ray Charles alongside pop sensation Tommy Roe, who still had a welding job with General Electric when he hit the Number One spot in 1962 with 'Sheila'. His follow-up Number One for the label, 'Dizzy', came seven years later.

Producer/manager/writer Lou Adler's Dunhill label was distributed through ABC until it was bought out in 1966. At this point the label's name was added to the letterhead, as the company officially became ABC Dunhill. The new company then set out on a concerted effort to expand the label's roster by signing rock, blues, and soul acts such as Steppenwolf, Three Dog Night, Steely Dan, BB King and Rufus.

Following Adler's decision to 'retire', ABC-Dunhill embarked on a programme of expansion with the acquisition of the Dot, Neighborhood and Blue Thumb labels in the '70s, but, with losses mounting, the parent company sold their music interests to MCA for upwards of $50 million. They kept several of the labels active for some years, but 1977 saw the last Number One acts in the US and UK on the ABC label. Other imprints now reside in the vaults of the Universal Music Group.

ACE

THE ORIGINAL ACE RECORDS WAS ESTABLISHED
IN AMERICA'S DEEP SOUTH IN 1955 BUT ROSE
TO PROMINENCE AS A RESULT OF ITS INVOLVE-
MENT IN THE R&B MUSIC OF NEW ORLEANS.
Founder Johnny Vincent – who launched his own Champion
label in Mississippi and worked for Speciality Records –
released AJ Collins' 'I Got The Blues For You' as the first Ace
record. The label's first success came with Huey 'Piano'
Smith, and this was followed by Joe Tex and Frankie Ford,
whose hit 'Sea Cruise' was produced by Vincent.

Dr John – the leader of New Orleans music for four
decades – began his career with Ace Records, when he
organised, played on and produced sessions as Mac
Rebennack. He remembers that many of the musicians had
to threaten Vincent to get their money: 'They had to pull a
gun to get paid, and this wasn't for their royalties.'

A merger with Vee Jay in the early '60s turned Ace into
a less-than-prestigious pop label before it disappeared as an
active record label. John Vincent, who was born John
Vincent Imbragulio and who died in February 2000, sold the
label to UK re-issues specialist Westside.

all around the world

ALL AROUND THE WORLD

ALL AROUND THE WORLD (AATW) RECORDS GREW OUT OF A THRIVING SPECIALIST DANCE MUSIC RETAILER BASED IN BLACKBURN. The dance label was formed in the early 1990s and flourished with a range of successful UK dance singles, featuring N'Trance and Kelly Llorenna alongside the *Clubland* compilation series, which are among the UK's best selling compilations titles.

Currently distributed through Universal, All Around The World, which uses the prefix Globe for its releases, has notched up charts hits for newer artists such as Flip & Fill, Dallas Superstars, Resonance Q and Ultrabeat.

AMERICAN RECORD CORPORATION

WHILE IT WAS NEVER ACTUALLY A RECORD COMPANY, the American Record Corporation (ARC) played an important part in the growth of America's recording industry by producing cheap records for small US labels for over 20 years.

The Scranton Button Company – founded in Scranton, Pennsylvania, in 1885 – expanded from the business of producing buttons and novelty goods into record pressing in the early '20s and acquired the Regal Records label. Links with the Plaza Music Company also brought Scranton the Banner and Domino labels, which was followed by the acquisition of an interest in the National Music Lovers' mail-order business and a pressing contract with the Oriole label.

Scranton expanded further in 1924, when the company bought the record division of Emerson Recording Laboratories, which included the Grey Gull label. By the end of the '20s, Scranton dominated America's dime-store record business, pressing for nearly a dozen labels, including Challenge, Homestead and Jewel.

In 1929, the company emerged with a new identity. By merging with the Cameo Record Corporation (owners of the Pathé label, which included the Regal operation along with the Perfect, Romeo and Oriole labels), Scranton formed the American Record Corporation, which remained Number One in the cheap record market that boomed in America in the '30s.

ARC purchased the Brunswick record operation from Warner Bros film studios in 1932, which gave them access to the important Brunswick label and Vocalion Records, featuring Delta blues star Robert Johnson. Two years later, ARC purchased the Columbia Phonograph Company, and established the operation as the world's largest pressing facility. However, in 1938 the Columbia Broadcasting System acquired ARC, sold off Brunswick and Vocalion and, as the new CBS record business grew, then transferred their record pressing to their own plant.

Without the CBS business, and after an ill-fated deal with the United States Record Corporation, Scranton's fortunes began to wane. The business finally came to an end in 1946, when the rapidly growing Capitol Records – a customer of ARC – exercised their option to buy the pressing plant for $2 million.

No 1
Singles -
Albums **2**

No 1
Singles -
Albums -

AMERICAN RECORDINGS

WHEN FORMER NEW YORK COLLEGE KID RICK RUBIN FELL OUT WITH RUSSELL SIMMONS, SPLITTING UP THE PARTNERSHIP THAT HAD SUCCESSFULLY SPAWNED DEF JAM RECORDS, he moved to California and created the Def America label. Focusing on metal and rock, Rubin launched his new LA-based label with Slayer in 1989, and later signed the likes of Masters Of Reality, The Geto Boys and The Black Crowes, along with British bands The Cult and Wolfsbane. Rubin, who produced The Beastie Boys and LL Cool J at Def Jam, expanded his production work to include Red Hot Chili Peppers, Mick Jagger and Sir Mix-A-Lot, while also launching the new dance/rap subsidiary Ill Records.

In 1993, Rubin decided to rename his label American Recordings, ceremoniously killing off the word Def – a word that he claimed had lost its radical edge – with a funeral procession and full coffin burial. The word had made it into slang dictionaries as meaning 'excellent'. The signing of Johnny Cash and Donovan to the label, alongside heavy metal and rap acts, gave American Recordings a particularly eclectic feel, unique in comparison with America's growing breed of specialist music labels.

Angel®

ANGEL

JUST A YEAR AFTER THE FOUNDING OF THE GRAMOPHONE COMPANY IN LONDON IN 1898, THE COMPANY'S RECORDS BEGAN TO BE ISSUED WITH THE FAMOUS RECORDING ANGEL TRADEMARK, DEVISED BY THEODORE BIRNBAUM. As the company's first label design, it gained worldwide prominence and, after the introduction of the legendary HMV dog-and-gramophone symbol, served as an alternative label in countries where the dog was considered to be an unclean animal.

Angel Records was formally established in America in the early 1950s – together with its sister Seraphim label – and was set up in North America as the major classical imprint by the Gramophone Company/EMI, where it had no rights to the HMV trademark. With the advent of centralised CD manufacturing and international bar codes, Angel was briefly employed as EMI's worldwide classical label. However, with the introduction of the EMI Classics label in the '90s it reverted to its American status, within Capitol Records, as the home of primarily crossover classical releases, featuring artists such as Sarah Brightman, Ravi Shankar and John McDermott.

No 1
Singles **13**
Albums **14**

No 1
Singles **5**
Albums **10**

APPLE

THE BEATLES LAUNCHED THE APPLE CORPS ORGANISATION IN 1968, WHICH ALONG WITH THE LABEL COMPRISED A LONDON BOUTIQUE, AN ARTS FOUNDATION AND AN ELECTRONICS DIVISION. Peter Asher, half of the duo Peter And Gordon and brother of actress (and later Paul McCartney's girlfriend) Jane Asher, was head of A&R. He signed James Taylor before moving to America, while bizarre inventor Magic Alex headed Zapple, the branch of the organisation which specialised in electronic technologies.

Each of the fab four involved themselves in projects for Apple, with artists such as Mary Hopkin, Hot Chocolate, Billy Preston, Badfinger, Grapefruit and The Plastic Ono Band, but The Beatles couldn't sign to the label because they were committed to EMI.

However, starting with the 1968 release 'Hey Jude', their records all carried the famous Apple logo, although they still had Parlophone numbers. Up until the mid '70s, singles and albums by The Beatles' – both as a group and as solo artists – were credited to Apple Records in both UK and US charts.

The Beatles' final live performance took place on the rooftop of Apple's offices in London's Savile Row to promote the *Let It Be* album, but the on-going dispute between group members over the management of their affairs led to the demise of the Apple label and the group's final dissolution in 1970.

Apple Corps still exists today, under the guidance of the group's original roadie, Neil Aspinall, and represents The Beatles' interests in merchandising, re-issues and television projects. The original Apple recordings, meanwhile, have been released under licence by EMI, after being unavailable for almost 20 years. The label re-appeared at the top of the charts in 2000 thanks to the release of the 20+ million-selling Beatles *1* album.

ARISTA

ARISTA RECORDS FIRST APPEARED IN 1975. Before then, the company had operated under Bell Records until ex-CBS Records executive Clive Davis was hired in 1974. Davis, who discovered Janis Joplin, Santana and Blood, Sweat And Tears for CBS, joined as head of Bell but changed the label's name to Arista (the name of the New York school system's honour society, of which Davis was a member). The company's musical direction also shifted from singles-orientated pop to middle-of-the-road music and rock.

Davis inherited singer/songwriter Barry Manilow and turned him into one the new breed of Arista stars. He was followed by hard-edged singer Patti Smith, evergreen group The Kinks and The Alan Parsons Project, featuring the former Pink Floyd engineer and the producer of Pilot and Steve Harley. At the end of the '70s, Arista was acquired by the German media giant BMG, through their long-standing German subsidiary Ariola, and a roster of new artists emerged on the label on both sides of the Atlantic.

Multi-million-selling superstar Whitney Houston progressed under Davis' personal guidance, which involved spending $300,000 on the recording of her first album. Also drafted onto the label were saxophonist Kenny G, soul diva Aretha Franklin and Ray Parker Jnr, all of whom were new American successes for the label. With ten weeks at the top of the charts, Houston's 1992 single 'I Will Always Love You' set a new record (which lasted until 1999) for the length of time that a song by a female artist remained at Number One in the UK.

No 1
Singles **24**
Albums **11**

No 1
Singles **9**
Albums **11**

ARISTA

In the midst of all this success, the duo Milli Vanilli appeared with a trio of US Number One singles, which helped to earn them the 1990 Grammy Award as Best New Artist. The revelation that they had not sung on any of their hits led to arguments between the act, their management and Arista, about who knew what, and the duo – Rob Pilatus and Fabrice Morvan – were forced to return their award.

While Slik, Showaddywaddy, The Thompson Twins and Lisa Stansfield carried the Arista banner in the UK, in America the emergence of solo star Annie Lennox, Canada's Crash Test Dummies and the Swedish band Ace Of Base brought new impetus to the label, following BMG's purchase of RCA Records in 1986. Halfway through the '90s, Arista was involved in two major joint venture deals – with R&B label La Face Records and leading rap company Bad Boy Records – which played a major part in making Arista America's hottest singles label in 1996.

In the UK, Arista oversaw the Northwest, Deconstruction, First Avenue and Dedicated labels. The label also distributed Heavenly, while in America million-selling artists such as Sarah McLachlan and a revitalised Santana were carrying the Arista banner.

Chart-topping star names to emerge under the new Arista regime include Avril Lavigne, Usher and Pink, plus Arista Nashville stars Alan Jackson and Brooks & Dunn.

US
No 1
Singles **5**
Albums **8**

UK
No 1
Singles -
Albums -

ASYLUM

ASYLUM

DAVID GEFFEN WAS PERSUADED TO SET UP ASYLUM RECORDS BY AHMET ERTEGUN, THE CHAIRMAN OF ATLANTIC RECORDS, who knew Geffen from his time as manager of Crosby, Stills And Nash. When Atlantic were offered Geffen's newest singer, Jackson Browne, Ertegun urged Geffen to start his own label and offered Atlantic's financial support.

Geffen, now a partner in Steven Spielberg's DreamWorks, started Asylum in 1971 with a budget of just $400,000. The label's first release was by Laura Nyro, which was followed in 1972 by the first Asylum albums from Jackson Browne, The Eagles and Joni Mitchell. Within a couple of years, Steve Ross, boss of Warner Communications, approached Geffen with an interest in buying Asylum. Geffen asked for $7 million, 'the biggest number I could think of'. He received $2 million in cash and the rest in WCI stock

Geffen remained president of the label, and in 1973 the Elektra label – which was already a part of Warner – was merged with Asylum under him. He continued to bolster Asylum (which boasted a floating prison door as its original design logo) with major artists such as Tom Waits, The Byrds, Linda Ronstadt and even Bob Dylan (albeit briefly), but he slashed the Elektra roster by dropping over 30 acts.

In 1975, Geffen moved into the film business before re-emerging with his own Geffen label, and gradually Asylum's image was overshadowed by the growing Elektra Entertainment Company, which operated the label as a country music outlet. However, in early 2000, with a new label design, Asylum was shifted into the country music operation of the sister company Warner Bros Records. Three years later the name Asylum was adopted by Curb Records as their Nashville-based country-music imprint and as home to star artist LeAnn Rimes.

No 1
Singles **8**
Albums **1**

No 1
Singles -
Albums -

ATCO

THE FORMATION AND LAUNCH OF ATCO IN 1957, AS A SUBSIDIARY OF ATLANTIC RECORDS, WAS ONE OF THE LAST TASKS TAKEN ON BY ORIGINAL ATLANTIC EXECUTIVE HERB ABRAMSON BEFORE HE LEFT THE COMPANY. Atco (which simply means Atlantic Company) was created as an alternative outlet for artists and records that didn't fit into Atlantic's well-established R&B/soul release schedule.

The first artist signed to the label was young white singer Bobby Darin. His first hit was 'Splish Splash', a record that, in his biography, *Rhythm And Blues*, Atlantic A&R man Jerry Wexler recalled disliking, while understanding its importance in establishing the new Atco label: 'After that record we were off to the races, and nobody knew he was white. Thank God we didn't have video then.'

In 1958, two years before the parent Atlantic company achieved the feat, Darin brought Atco its first Number One with 'Mack The Knife', produced by Atlantic boss Ahmet Ertegun. In 1962, the label made a little more history when English jazz clarinetist Acker Bilk became the first British artist to reach Number One in the American pop singles chart with 'Stranger On The Shore'.

After Atco was up and running, Abramson parted company with Atlantic and went on to launch the Triumph, Blaze and Festival labels. He died in November 1999, at the age of 82.

Husband-and-wife team Sonny And Cher – the latter's 1998 solo hit 'Believe' being Britain's greatest-ever-selling single by a female artist – topped the charts in America and the UK in 1965 with 'I Got You, Babe', although outside the US the record appeared on the Atlantic label.

Meanwhile, American rock group Iron Butterfly were joined on Atco by the roster of artists signed to Robert Stigwood's RSO stable, and during the late '60s and early '70s Cream, Blind Faith, Derek And The Dominoes, Eric Clapton and The Bee Gees all appeared on the label. Finally, British band Yes were the last Atco album chart-toppers in 1987, and in 1990 Sweet Sensation became the label's final act to have a Number One single. The label's presence was gradually reduced from being a front-line operation to become only an imprint for Atco catalogue releases.

ATLANTIC

50 YEARS AFTER ATLANTIC RECORDS EARNED ITS FIRST HIT RECORD, WITH STICK McGHEE'S INTRIGUINGLY TITLED 'DRINKING WINE SPO-DEE-O-DEE', the label was celebrating the success of current signings The Corrs, the UK's best-selling album artists in 1998.

McGhee's initial success came a year after the label had been formed in New York by son of a Turkish diplomat Ahmet Ertegun and student Herb Abramson, with the help of a $10,000 loan from Ertegun's dentist. Abramson was a part-time producer for the National Records label, where he worked with Joe Turner and Billy Eckstine, while Ertegun was an equally avid collector of jazz records, which he harvested from Waxie Maxie Silver's Quality Music shop in Washington, DC.

Establishing the label in 1947, the pair decided on the name Atlantic for their East Coast jazz imprint because there was already a popular West Coast jazz company called Pacific. In those early days, Ertegun – who remains co-chairman of Atlantic 50 years after founding the label – learned the two most important stages in being successful in the record business: make a great record and then get it played on radio.

After their first taste of success, the label added more artists to its roster, and also recruited Billboard reviewer Jerry Wexler to join the team in 1953 as A&R man and producer. In return for an initial investment of just over $2,000, Wexler received a 13% stake in the company, which later increased to 30%.

Atlantic soon became the leading R&B label, thanks to recordings by The Coasters, The Drifters and Ray Charles, whom Ertegun credited as being the man who taught him about making records. He had bought the singer's contract from Swing Time Records for $2,000.

Ertegun, Abramson and Wexler not only discovered talented artists and made popular records; theirs also proved to be one of the few labels around to reward its artists properly. As Ertegun told Joe Smith in his book *Off The Record*, 'They made a hit record, they got a decent royalty and they got paid on time.' In order to pay their artists, and in order to make a decent living themselves, Atlantic's trio of executives released three records each month, of which they then had to sell a total of 60,000 copies to cover their costs.

In 1955, another Ertegun joined the team – Ahmet's elder brother, Nesuhi – and signed jazz artists The Modern Jazz Quartet, John Coltrane, Charlie Mingus and Roland Kirk to the label's roster.

Meanwhile, Ertegun Jr and Wexler focused on America's fast-growing interest in rock and pop music. They even tried to poach Elvis Presley from Sun for $30,000, but they lost out to RCA's bid.

Soul group The Drifters had the honour of being the act to take the famous red-and-black Atlantic label to Number One for the first time in 1960 with their single 'Save The Last Dance For Me'. This heralded a golden decade of soul music for Atlantic, thanks to their links with the Memphis-based Stax label and Otis Redding, and their direct signings Wilson Pickett, Aretha Franklin, Solomon Burke, Percy Sledge and Sam And Dave.

The '60s also saw Atlantic move into contemporary rock. Although they passed on Bob Dylan, the label went on to launch Crosby, Stills, Nash And Young and Led Zeppelin, who – together with their heavyweight manager, Peter Grant – made things more difficult by deciding never to release any singles and to issue a fourth album that featured neither band name nor title.

Near the end of the glorious '60s, when the company issued the chart-topping *Woodstock Festival* album on its Cotillion subsidiary, Atlantic came under new ownership when the Erteguns and Wexler sold out to Warner-Seven Arts for $17.5 million. Wexler explained his reasons for the sale in his biography, *Rhythm And Blues*: 'We sold for the American dream: capital gains. My idea was to live where it was sunny, and in some vague way I thought I could phone it in.' Two years later, Kinney bought Warner-Seven Arts and created Warner Communications, which subsequently merged with Time Inc to form the conglomerate Time Warner, Inc.

No 1
Singles **37**
Albums **22**

No 1
Singles **8**
Albums **10**

ATLANTIC

While Wexler left for his beloved Miami (but not before voicing his opposition to Atlantic's proposed funding of the budding Asylum Records), Ahmet Ertegun set about the day-to-day running of the Atlantic Corporation of the '70s and finding new talent. One of his first new signings were The Rolling Stones, in a deal which turned out to be one of the most important in Atlantic's history. Appearing with their own tongue logo, The Stones notched up a host of hit singles and albums for Atlantic, paving the way for even greater success for the label throughout the '70s, with acts like Chic, The Detroit Spinners, Average White Band, Foreigner and, in America, Swedish pop sensations Abba. A decade later, Atlantic added a new breed of stars with Bette Midler, AC/DC, INXS, Genesis and Phil Collins.

Today, Atlantic Records boasts a new roster of million-selling acts, including Hootie & The Blowfish, Stone Temple Pilots, Collective Soul, Brandy, Jewel and Lil' Kim. Sugar Ray and Matchbox 20 appear on their Lava subsidiary, along with award-winning Irish group The Corrs, via 143 Records (a joint-venture label with prize-winning producer David Foster), while reggae star Sean Paul emerged from the label's link with VP Records. The label that was founded over half a century ago by a man who composed songs under the name Nugetre (Ertegun backwards) has gone on to become almost as famous as any of its artists.

ATO

MILLION-SELLING AMERICAN SINGER DAVE MATTHEWS LAUNCHED ATO (ACCORDING TO OUR) RECORDS IN 2000 IN PARTNERSHIP WITH HIS MANAGER, Coran Capshaw, and retained tour manager Michael McDonald and band associate Chris Tetzeli to run the label.

While Matthews remains signed to RCA Records, his New York-based label has signed UK star David Gray for America, alongside Patty Griffin and Ben Kweller, and Matthews has gone on record to explain his commitment to the label saying; 'If there is something I come across that I feel very strongly about, that's when its great to have a label.'

No 1
Singles **1**
Albums -

No 1
Singles **1**
Albums **1**

AVCO

ARTISTS, PRODUCERS, WRITERS AND A&R MEN HUGO PERETTI AND LUIGI CREATORE ENJOYED HUGE SUCCESS BEFORE STARTING UP THE AVCO LABEL IN THE LATE '60s. The two American-born entrepreneurs worked at Mercury Records before buying Roulette Records in 1957 (which they sold two years later) and going on to work at RCA with Sam Cooke, The Tokens and Elvis Presley.

Peretti and Creatore set up the label together with legendary film producer Joseph Levine, and it went on to become a success, mainly thanks to soul group The Stylistics. The band notched up over a dozen hits for the label before moving on to Hugo and Luigi's own H&L label, together with Van McCoy. Creatore later retired to Florida and Peretti died in 1986.

AVEX

JAPAN'S LEADING DANCE COMPILATION COMPANY DURING THE '90s, AVEX LATER BRANCHED OUT INTO BUILDING A ROSTER OF HIGHLY SUCCESSFUL LOCAL ARTISTS, FOCUSING ON J-POP AND DANCE. Set up as a CD distribution operation in 1988 by Tom Yoda and claiming a market share of 15.3% of the world's second-largest market for recorded music in 1998, the company – which has unsuccessfully attempted international expansion – achieved further success with million-sellers Globe, Every Little Thing, Ayumi Hamasaki and Backstreet Boys, under a licence from Zomba which expired in 2001. They went public in 1998, and raised over $31 million on the first day of trading on the stock market. In 1999, they moved into the lucrative Chinese-language market, opening a subsidiary in Taiwan and confirmed their status as Japan's most successful independent music company, with interests in night clubs, restaurants and artist management. The company – which entered the lucrative American market in 2000 with the launch of Avex Experience America – posted its first ever half year losses in September 2002 and slipped from its position as Japan's leading independent.

ACE UK – see Chiswick

ADDITIVE – see Positiva

AFTERMATH – see Interscope

ALADDIN – see Island

ALL PLATINUM – see Sugar Hill

AMY – see Arista

ANTI – see Epitaph

ANTILLES – see Island

ARGO – see Chess

ARIOLA – see Arista

ARISTOCRAT – see Chess

AUDIUM – see Koch

AUTUMN – see Warner Bros

AZULI – see Island

No 1
Singles **4**
Albums **6**

No 1
Singles **2**
Albums -

ENTERTAINMENT

BAD BOY

HARLEM-BORN SEAN COMBS BEGAN HIS CAREER IN THE MUSIC BUSINESS AT UPTOWN RECORDS, WHERE, AT JUST 21 YEARS OF AGE, HE DISCOVERED MARY J BLIGE AND NOTORIOUS BIG BEFORE BEING FIRED. This turn of events gave him the incentive and opportunity to form his own record company, Bad Boy, in 1992. Over the next few years, Combs produced projects by Blige and Notorious (who had been forced to change his name from Biggie Smalls for legal reasons), found himself elected one of New York's Smartest 100 and was named Man Of The Year by the Institute Of African-American Music in 1996.

As head of Bad Boy Entertainment, Combs signed Faith Evans and Total to the roster. He also signed himself, under the name Puff Daddy, and releases his records under the Puff Daddy imprint. His tribute records following Notorious BIG's murder in Los Angeles – the single 'I'll Be Missing You' and the album *No Way Out* – notched up combined sales of over five million, while Notorious' own last album, *Life After Death*, sold six million copies.

Bad Boy and Puff Daddy were thus established at the forefront of rap music, and Combs had a clear vision of the future for his company: 'Bad Boy will go down in history as one of the most important, diverse and powerful conglomerates. I want Bad Boy to be a big name.' Combs obtained further funding and increased status for Bad Boy in 1996 when BMG's Arista Records acquired 50% of the company. In 2002, Combs ended his association with Arista's BMG and linked briefly with Epic (where he again hit the US number one spot) before concluding a deal with Universal Records.

No 1
Singles -
Albums -

No 1
Singles -
Albums **4**

BEGGARS BANQUET GROUP

AFTER OVER TWO DECADES IN BUSINESS, BEGGARS BANQUET HAS GROWN FROM A SINGLE RECORD SHOP TO BECOME ONE OF THE UK'S LEADING INDEPENDENT RECORD COMPANIES, boasting an annual turnover in excess of £15 million from a roster of nearly 40 artists signed to six different labels.

Martin Mills and Nick Austin initially used the name Beggars Banquet for a mobile disco before opening their first shop in London's Earls Court in 1974. Further shops, promotions and management companies followed, until the Beggars Banquet record label was born in 1977 to launch punk band The Lurkers.

Financial problems required them to sign a deal with WEA, but then Tubeway Army topped the charts, heralding the arrival of Gary Numan and securing the label's future. Through new labels Situation Two and 4AD, a succession of bands – including The Charlatans, The Pixies, The Cocteau Twins and M/A/R/R/S (who reached Number One with 'Pump Up The Volume') – reinforced the successes of Banquet acts Bauhaus, The Cult and The Fall, establishing the company at the forefront of the '80s indie boom.

With the emergence of dance and rave music, Beggars Banquet introduced the XL label, which released records by Basement Jaxx and Prodigy, whose album *Fat Of The Land* became the most successful independent album in the world. The labels Mantra, Mo'Wax, Locked On and Wiija (featuring Cornershop) complete the Beggars Banquet group of outlets, which are still presided over by founder and chairman Mills. As Badly Drawn Boy and The White Stripes brought new success to the group, Mills confirmed his company's position: 'We don't aim to make huge profits. We just aim to put out great music.'

No 1
Singles **6**
Albums -

No 1
Singles **13**
Albums **3**

BELL

COLPIX, THE RECORD ARM OF COLUMBIA PICTURES – WHICH HAS NO CONNECTION WITH COLUMBIA/CBS RECORDS – WAS ESTABLISHED IN 1960. The company sowed the seeds of the successful Bell label in 1964 when they took over the Bell/Amy/Mala group of labels, previously owned by children's music entrepreneur Al Massler.

Under the guidance of Larry Utall, founder of Madison Records, the labels moved into pop music with the likes of Del Shannon and James And Bobby Purify. These labels were eventually gathered under the name Bell, although when The Box Tops topped the US charts in 1967 with 'The Letter' they did so on the Mala label. During the next ten years, the Bell label was home to a host of chart-topping acts on both sides of the Atlantic.

Television stars The Partridge Family started the ball rolling in 1970, and were followed by Dawn and Barry Manilow, while in the UK Edison Lighthouse took Bell to the Number One spot in the same year. Ex-Partridge Family member David Cassidy, Gary Glitter and teenybop idols The Bay City Rollers confirmed Bell's status as one of pop music's hottest labels.

Bell maintained a presence in the UK for several years, despite Utall's departure and Clive Davis' decision to change the company's name to Arista in 1975. In 1976, Showaddywaddy's only Number One, 'Under The Moon Of Love', became the last chart-topper on the Bell label.

No 1
Singles -
Albums -

No 1
Singles 1
Albums 1

BIG LIFE

FORMED AS A MANAGEMENT AND RECORD COMPANY BY TIM PARRY AND JAZZ SUMMERS, a member of the team which managed Wham!, Big Life came into being in 1987, with producers/artists Cold Cut among their début acts. The group's vocalist, Yazz, went on to solo success with the label, and also married Summers. Big Life were one of the first UK labels to involve themselves with rap, with the group London Possee, and forged links with the US label Tommy Boy to release De La Soul and Naughty By Nature in the UK. They also launched Blue Pearl and The Orb.

While the management company successfully looked after Brit Award winners Lisa Stansfield and producer Youth, a major interest in the Big Life record label was acquired by distributors Polydor. However, in 1994 Summers bought back Big Life Records, although it went into voluntary liquidation in 1998. Once again, the company focused on its management operation, which included managing The Verve until their split in 1999.

Blanco Y Negro

BLANCO Y NEGRO

IN 1983, GEOFF TRAVIS, THE FOUNDER OF ROUGH TRADE RECORDS, WENT ON TO SET UP THE LABEL BLANCO Y NEGRO WITHIN THE UK MAJOR RECORD COMPANY WEA RECORDS. The duo Everything But The Girl, along with former Creation act The Jesus And Mary Chain, maintained the label's profile for more than a decade. With Travis maintaining his A&R role within the operation, Scottish singer Eddi Reader and Welsh band Catatonia joined the roster in the mid '90s and continued Blanco Y Negro's chart success. In 2003, former Catatonia singer Cerys Matthews re-emerged on the label with her début solo album.

No 1
Singles -
Albums -

No 1
Singles **1**
Albums -

BLUE HORIZON

VETERAN BLUES SUPPORTER MIKE VERNON AND HIS BROTHER RICHARD LAUNCHED BLUE HORIZON IN THE MID '60s AS AN OUTLET FOR RECORDINGS FROM INDEPENDENT AMERICAN BLUES LABELS, before launching the careers of emerging British blues acts such as John Mayall, Chicken Shack and the original Fleetwood Mac. At an early stage in the label's life, Vernon forged an agreement with Sire Records' boss Seymour Stein to have material by Blue Horizon artists released in America. The deal left Stein with shared ownership of the Blue Horizon label, which he still uses in America for selected releases.

Between March 1968 and August 1969, Fleetwood Mac released three chart albums for Blue Horizon and the haunting chart-topping single 'Albatross' before they switched to Reprise. Vernon then axed the label in order to focus on production work with the likes of Focus and Bloodstone. He revived Blue Horizon in 1988, however, and released contemporary blues acts such as Lazy Lester and The De Luxe Blues Band, while also forming the Code Blue label.

Now, over 30 years after the inception of the original Blue Horizon label, Vernon continues to record new releases for the Blue Horizon imprint in the UK. The original catalogue recordings are available through re-issue specialists.

No 1
Singles -
Albums **1**

No 1
Singles -
Albums **1**

BLUE NOTE

IN 1999, BLUE NOTE RECORDS CELEBRATED 60 YEARS OF BEING ONE OF THE WORLD'S PREMIER JAZZ LABELS. Founded by jazz fan Alfred Lions, whose first release was by pianists Meade Lux Lewis and Albert Ammons in 1939, Blue Note's catalogue features the recordings of jazz giants such as Thelonious Monk, Miles Davis, John Coltrane, Art Blakey, Herbie Hancock, Horace Silver and Dexter Gordon, among many others.

Blue Note was one of the first labels to focus on logo design and cover art-work, with Lions' partner Francis Wolf being responsible for the atmospheric black-and-white artists' photographs. Lions retired in 1967, just after the label was bought by Liberty, while Wolf worked on at the label until his death in 1971.

After EMI purchased Liberty in 1979, as part of United Artists, the label was phased out until 1985, when it was re-launched as part of EMI's New York-based Manhattan Records, with Bobby McFerrin and Stanley Jordan as its premier artists. Lions died in 1987, although Blue Note later re-emerged as a jazz giant with artists such as Dianne Reeves, Lena Horne, Cassandra Wilson and Mose Allison. In 1994, the label released the crossover hit 'Cantaloop' by Us3, but 2002 brought the historic jazz label its biggest ever commercial success thanks to multi-Grammy-award winner Norah Jones.

BMG ENTERTAINMENT

THE GERMAN MEDIA GIANT BERTELSMANN BECAME ONE OF THE WORLD'S MAJOR MUSIC COMPANIES WHEN IT ACQUIRED THE HISTORIC AMERICAN COMPANY RCA RECORDS IN 1986, which it put alongside its existing Ariola and Arista labels to form BMG (the Bertelsmann Music Group).

Originally formed in the 1830s, Bertelsmann prospered after the end of World War Two and became an international force in books, magazines, printing, film and television, while also controlling the Ariola/Eurodisc music operations. The American company Arista Records was acquired in 1979, and RCA Records – which had been set up by the Victor company in 1929 – was bought in 1986. Coincidentally, RCA had tried unsuccessfully to acquire Ariola/Arista in 1985 before itself being taken over by General Electric, who subsequently sold it to Bertelsmann.

BMG Entertainment operates the RCA, Arista,J, Private Music and Windham Hill labels, BMG Conifer classical division (including RCA Red Seal, RCA Victor and Melodiya) and, until December 2002, had a minority interest in the independent company Zomba. Then BMG bought the world's top indie for $2.7 billion and Zomba's founding father, Clive Calder, left the company.

No 1
Singles -
Albums -

No 1
Singles -
Albums **1**

BRONZE

GERRY BRON'S LONG INVOLVEMENT WITH THE UK MUSIC BUSINESS – INCLUDING A TRACK RECORD OF WORKING FOR RECORD COMPANIES, music publishers and management companies – culminated in the inauguration of Bronze Records in the mid '70s. The label operated alongside the Roundhouse Studios complex, which was run by Bron and his wife Lillian and was located on the same site in Chalk Farm as London's famous '70s concert venue, a former railway turntable and depot.

Bronze was linked with EMI distribution, and ranked among the leading British independents as Manfred Mann's Earth Band brought the label UK chart success (although their US Number One 'Blinded By The Light' was released on Warner Bros).

Heavy metal supergroup Motörhead – led by Lemmy and boasting a 126-decibel live show – were the label's next success, along with female rock group Girlschool and Sally Oldfield, sister of Mike, the creator of *Tubular Bells*. Lemmy's former group, Hawkwind, also made a brief appearance on Bronze in 1980.

In 1987, the Bronze catalogue was bought by Roy Richards, who included it in his PR company, which was later acquired by Castle Communications, and which in turn was bought by the Sanctuary Group in 2000. Meanwhile, the Bronze trademark was bought by producer Pete Winkleman in 1990, who closed down Bronze Records, after enjoying brief success with The Wildhearts in the early '90s.

Founder of the original label, Gerry Bron, re-acquired the rights to the name and trademark of Bronze Records in 2000 and, in partnership with his son Richard, is planning a re-launch of the label with new acts such as Cube, James Blundell and Space Junky.

BRUNSWICK

PIANO MANUFACTURERS WERE RESPONSIBLE FOR THE LAUNCHING OF THE BRUNSWICK LABEL ON BOTH SIDES OF THE ATLANTIC, but with seven years separating the two events. Brunswick-Balke-Collender started the Brunswick label in America in 1916, with classical conductor Arturo Toscanini among its first signings, while Chappell Pianos launched Brunswick in the UK in 1923.

Success in America came in 1928 with Al Jolson and 'Sonny Boy', the first big hit from talking pictures. This was followed by hits from Bing Crosby and Fred Astaire before the label was caught up in a extraordinary round of acquisitions. The company was purchased by Warner Bros in 1930, and this was followed with its sale to ARC (the American Record Corporation) within the space of a year. This move established the Brunswick Record Corporation, added artists such as The Mills Brothers, The Andrews Sisters and Harry James, and saw the acquisition of the Columbia and Okeh subsidiaries. CBS bought the label in 1938.

Following CBS's decision to axe the label, Brunswick moved on to Decca US in 1942. Decca re-activated the label with the likes of Jackie Wilson (whose 1957 hit 'Reet Petite' was written by Berry Gordy, a man who would later create the Motown empire), The Crickets (released on Coral in the UK) and teen star Brenda Lee.

Label chief Nat Tarnopol, who was also Wilson's manager, bought Brunswick in 1969 and ran it alongside his Dakar label. However, because of his business methods he and his fellow directors were charged with (but later acquitted of) fraud and conspiracy.

No 1
Singles **2**
Albums -

No 1
Singles **6**
Albums -

BRUNSWICK

Brunswick's final move was to MCA, where The Chi-Lites brought new success to the label. Their 1972 US Number One came 15 years after Brunswick's only other US chart-topper, by The Crickets, in 1957. The label was finally closed down in 1984.

At the same time, Brunswick UK went through a similar scenario, with Count Antonio de Bosdari acquiring the label in 1927 before selling it on to Duophone a year later. The US deals involving Warner Bros and ARC included the Brunswick UK company, which ended up with Decca UK in 1932, where it was used as the imprint for US releases such as Bill Haley's earliest rock 'n' roll hits 'Shake, Rattle And Roll' and the chart-topping song 'Rock Around The Clock'.

Through a deal involving Decca US, The Who released six UK hit singles on Brunswick. However, as in the US, the label was headed towards oblivion, with the expiration of Decca UK's deal with US Brunswick in 1979 and MCA's acquisition of the American Brunswick in 1984.

BUDDAH

No 1
Singles **2**
Albums -

No 1
Singles -
Albums -

BUDDAH

FORMER CAMEO-PARKWAY EXECUTIVE NEIL BOGART, WHO HAD BEEN A RECORDING ARTIST UNDER THE NAME NEIL SCOTT, ESTABLISHED BUDDAH RECORDS IN NEW YORK IN 1967, in partnership with Art Kass and Artie Ripp. The new label immediately hit the big time, with bubblegum hits from 1910 Fruitgum Company and Ohio Express, along with The Lemon Pipers and Lou Christie, all of which were distributed through Pye Records in the UK. In the label's first year, its sales were estimated to have exceeded $5.8 million.

According to Bogart (who later suffered from major drug abuse), bubblegum pop was a response to the heavy, drug-influenced rock of the late '60s, 'giving the kids something to identify with that is clean, fresh and happy'. Bogart signed folk singer Melanie, and benefited from her inspirational appearance at 1969's original Woodstock festival. He later added the Kama Sutra label, which became the home of The Lovin' Spoonful. Before leaving the label in 1974, Bogart also introduced The Edwin Hawkins Singers, Curtis Mayfield and Motown stalwarts Gladys Knight And The Pips to Buddah. Despite continuing success with Knight and with spoof rock 'n' roll band Sha Na Na, Buddah never again hit the high spots, and the label's final owners, New York slide and projector manufacturer Viewplex, went bankrupt in 1976.

BENSON – see Zomba

BETHLEHEM – see King

BIG BROTHER – see Sony

BIG CAT – see V2

BIG TOP – see London

BLACK SWAN – see Island

BLUE BIRD – see RCA

BLUE THUMB – see ABC Dunhill

BOARDWALK – see Casablanca

BRENTWOOD – see Zomba

BROTHER – see Reprise

BUENA VISTA – see Hollywood

 No 1
Singles -
Albums -

 No 1
Singles 4
Albums -

C

CAMEO-PARKWAY

LAUNCHED IN PHILADELPHIA BY SONGWRITERS BERNIE LOWE AND KAL MANN IN 1956, Cameo Records and its Parkway subsidiary brought fame and fortune to an ex-chicken-plucker and gave the world a brand new dance. Chubby Checker, a poultry worker named Ernest Evans, was named after the style of Fats Domino. After being signed by Mann, he recorded Hank Ballard's 'The Twist' in 1960.

The label's close association with Dick Clark's *American Bandstand* TV show first brought Checker to Cameo-Parkway's attention when he was recruited to sing impressions on Clark's idea of a Christmas card in the form of a record. Checker told Joe Smith in *Off The Record* what happened after that: 'Kal Mann came up to me and said "We got this record called 'The Twist'. I think we can put a little dance to it and you can show people how it's done." I said "OK." We did it in three takes.'

Cameo-Parkway were at the heart of Philadelphia's prime position in American late-'50s pop music, launching hits for Charlie Grace, The Orlons, Dee Dee Sharp, Big Dee Irwin and Bobby Rydell, along with The Tymes, whose 1963 Number One 'So Much In Love' was the last chart-topper of the Lowe/Mann era.

The duo sold Cameo-Parkway in 1963, and within a year, as the British beat boom took off in America, Cameo-Parkway's fortunes took a downward turn. They had one last big US hit in 1966, '96 Tears' by the oddly named ? And The Mysterians, who were signed by label president Neil Bogart.

Following the closure of the label as a going concern, Cameo-Parkway's catalogue was acquired in 1968 by The Rolling Stones' former manager Allen Klein, who would be at the centre of the Lennon/McCartney management dispute that would ultimately lead to The Beatles splitting up a year later.

CAPITOL

LONG BEFORE ARTISTS LIKE PRINCE OR MADONNA HIT UPON THE IDEA OF STARTING UP THEIR OWN RECORD LABELS, two American songwriters and a record retailer teamed up in 1942 to establish the first major record company to be based on America's West Coast. Composers Johnny Mercer and Buddy De Sylva met for lunch with Glenn Wallichs in Hollywood's Lucey's restaurant for lunch, and with De Sylva's investment of $10,000 they sowed the seeds that grew into Capitol Records.

The company began life as Liberty Records, but contractual problems forced a re-think and the name Capitol was chosen, along with a label design featuring four stars around a domed roof. Speaking in 1967, Mercer – winner of four composer's Oscars – stated: 'There were so many talented people coming along; a new record company was inevitable. That Capitol turned out to be the big one was a matter of luck, timing and being in Hollywood.'

The new Capitol label was hit immediately by a wartime shortage of shellac, the raw material used for making discs. They overcame this problem by buying up old records from dealers and collectors for six cents a pound and converting them into new discs. Wallichs' experience as a retailer persuaded Capitol to establish their own distribution branches around America rather than choosing to use the existing independent arrangement.

Ella Mae Morse's 'Cow Cow Boogie', one of Capitol's first six releases in 1942, reached Number One in the chart at a time when recording music was made even more difficult by a two-year strike called by the American Federation Of Musicians. Much of Capitol's progress came about as a result of adopting a new way of conducting business, which included the idea of giving away free promotional records to disc jockeys, recording masters on magnetic tape and issuing records at all three available speeds.

In 1947, the label signed a three-year deal with Decca which gave the British company the rights to release Capitol material in the UK. Mercer left in the same year to focus on songwriting, and very soon afterwards De Sylva retired due to ill

CAPITOL

health. The label's investment in new talent brought artists such as Peggy Lee, Tex Ritter, Stan Kenton, Nat King Cole and – in 1953 – Frank Sinatra, who produced 13 Top Five albums for Capitol between 1954 and 1961 before leaving to form his own Reprise label.

In November 1952, the UK music paper *New Musical Express* launched the first British singles chart and Capitol's Al Martino was first to top the new chart with 'Hope In My Heart'. Seven years earlier, Nat King Cole's first group, The King Cole Trio, were at Number One in the first *Billboard* Best-Selling Record Album Top Five chart in March 1945 with *Collection Of Favorites*.

By 1955, Capitol had become America's fourth most successful record label, behind the established triumvirate of Columbia, RCA Victor and Decca. This achievement attracted the interest of British record giant EMI, who were searching for an American arm. They bought a controlling interest in Capitol for $8.5 million, and in London EMI Chairman Sir Joseph Lockwood commented that he heard someone at Capitol saying: 'Next week we'll have men with umbrellas and bowler hats telling us what to do.'

Wallichs remained president of EMI's new US operation, a position which he was to hold until 1972, and in 1956 Capitol moved into its new revolutionary head-quarters at Hollywood and Vine: the landmark Capitol Tower, a 13-floor building designed to resemble a stack of records. In the same year, Capitol earned its first UK and US Number One with Tennessee Ernie Ford's '16 Tons', which was closely followed by million-selling acts such as Dean Martin, Les Paul and Mary Ford, along-side C&W stars Merle Haggard and Buck Owens. Meanwhile, the newly-acquired classical Angel label featured opera diva Maria Callas.

When rock 'n' roll and a new style of pop music emerged, Capitol responded by signing Gene Vincent, The Kingston Trio and The Beach Boys, but they initially missed out on their parent company's biggest stars by refusing to release the first recordings by The Beatles. Pressure from EMI forced a change of heart, however, and Capitol went on to claim nearly 40 US Number One singles and albums by John, Paul, George

No 1
Singles **51**
Albums **45**

No 1
Singles **14**
Albums **5**

CAPITOL

and Ringo. The subsidiary Tower label was re-activated in 1964 and notched up just one US chart-topper from Manchester's Freddie And The Dreamers.

The label's chart action throughout the '60s attracted a roster of newer acts such as The Band, Helen Reddy, Anne Murray, Grand Funk Railroad, Steve Miller, Glen Campbell and the UK's Pink Floyd, who maintained Capitol's presence before handing over to the likes of Bob Seger, Dr Hook, Maze, Tavares, Natalie Cole and Heart. Capitol launched the alternative labels EMI America and Manhattan as part of its overall American operation, and in 1979 the parent company EMI – soon to be taken over by Thorn – took full control of the growing Capitol Industries and made it part of a new division: EMI Music Worldwide.

As new labels and new music emerged in the '80s, Capitol ceased to be a powerhouse of American music. However, a re-invigorated label emerged in the next decade, releasing material by the likes of Bonnie Raitt, MC Hammer, Tina Turner, Crowded House and The Beastie Boys, along with Duran Duran and Paul McCartney, who re-signed to the label. These artists returned the famous Capitol name to the headlines up to and beyond its 50th anniversary. Its 1991 position as America's Number Two Pop Album Label was its highest position since *Billboard* began tracking such chart information in the early '70s.

While the label struggled to introduce new British pop artists, such as Robbie Williams and Geri Halliwell, one man has so dominated Capitol's performance during the past decade that he was named the biggest-selling male singer in America's pop history. Country music star Garth Brooks achieved total sales close to 100 million since releasing his début album for Capitol in 1989. He was second in the list of all-time best sellers behind The Beatles (who, ironically, went on to amass sales of 120+ million after having been originally shunned by Capitol in 1963). Brooks, Elvis's daughter, Lisa Marie, and UK bands Radiohead and Coldplay, have maintained Capitol's chart presence in recent years.

No 1
Singles -
Albums **1**

No 1
Singles -
Albums -

CAPRICORN

IN 1969, FORMER MANAGER OF SOUL STARS OTIS REDDING AND SAM AND DAVE, PHIL WALDEN, STARTED UP HIS CAPRICORN LABEL IN MACON, GEORGIA, at around the same time that he persuaded Duane Allman to form The Allman Brothers Band. Capricorn was initially distributed by Atlantic, and The Allmans' début album appeared on its subsidiary Atco label before they switched to Capricorn in 1971. Other Capricorn acts included Elvin Bishop, Liv Ullman and Alex Taylor.

The label then switched to a deal with Warner Bros Records and focused on promoting The Allman Brothers, who split and reformed several times following the death of Duane Allman in 1971. Capricorn went out of business in 1980, but Walden – who retained the rights to the name and recordings of Capricorn Records – re-emerged with a joint venture deal with the Polygram-owned label Mercury Records. After Polygram was bought by Universal, a 50% share in Capricorn was held by Island/Def Jam, and the label achieved new success with the band 311.

No 1
Singles **7**
Albums **4**

No 1
Singles -
Albums -

CASABLANCA

IN 1973, SOON AFTER LEAVING BUDDAH RECORDS, NEIL BOGART TOOK TO CALIFORNIA AND SET UP CASABLANCA RECORDS, linking up with Warner Bros Records to distribute his new label. Within 18 months, however, the label – named after the famous Humphrey Bogart (no relation) movie – was floundering without a single hit, despite the signing of KISS. However, after adopting independent status, Casablanca hit the big-time with Donna Summer, Parliament and KISS, and Bogart was moved to start up Casablanca's sister movie company. In 1977, his success attracted a successful bid from Polygram, who acquired 50% of the company.

Bogart's reputation as a man of excess resulted in him employing over 200 members of staff (to many of whom he gave expensive cars), having the offices modelled to resemble Rick's Café in *Casablanca* (complete with stuffed camel) and ensuring a plentiful supply of drugs.

The label's record sales ran into millions, after being boosted by disco act The Village People, and they were complemented by the success of films such as *Midnight Express*. However, Bogart became carried away with this success, and despite declining sales boasted an artists roster of 100 acts.

In an attempt to stop the rot as Casablanca's fortunes waned, Polygram bought the outstanding half of the company and forced Bogart out in exchange for a reported $15 million. Ironically, after Bogart left the label hit the top spot in America with Captain And Tennille, Lipps Inc and Irene Cara, while Casablanca Filmworks became the basis for the successful film company Polygram Pictures, which made the movies *Missing* and *Four Weddings And A Funeral*.

Bogart set up one more label (Boardwalk, in 1980) and produced one more hit act (Joan Jett) before dying of cancer in 1982.

In 2003, Universal Music, which inherited the Casablanca name and label with its acquisition of Polygram, announced that a new joint venture label to be created with former Sony Music head Tommy Mottola would be called Casablanca Records.

Mottola was quoted as saying he 'wanted to use the name Casablanca to acknowledge the entrepreneurial spirit of the original label', which folded in 1984.

CHARISMA

No 1
Singles **2**
Albums -

No 1
Singles -
Albums **7**

CHARISMA

FORMER BRITISH JOURNALIST TONY 'STRAT' STRATTON-SMITH
FOUNDED CHARISMA IN 1969 AND FILLED THE ROSTER WITH THE
BANDS WHICH HE MANAGED, such as The Nice, Van Der Graaf Generator
and, ultimately, Genesis, which featured two solo stars of the future: Peter Gabriel
and Phil Collins.

Lindisfarne, Rick Wakeman and Clifford T Ward were joined at Charisma (which
also boasted a book publishing house) by Stratton-Smith's own oddball favourites,
including Monty Python's Flying Circus, cricket commentator John Arlott and poet
John Betjeman. Sex Pistols manager Malcolm McLaren and John Lennon's son
Julian were among the last artists signed to Charisma by Strat before his death in
March 1987 The label was bought by Virgin in 1984, and in 1990 they launched it
as a second label in the US, featuring artists such as Maxi Priest and T'Pau.

CHERRY RED

INDEPENDENT PUNK LABEL CHERRY RED STARTED LIFE AS A CONCERT-PROMOTION BUSINESS, FOUNDED IN 1978 IN GREAT MALVERN, WORCESTERSHIRE. Iain McNay was originally one of the partners in Cherry Red Promotions – named after a track on the Groundhogs' *Split* album – and when he became involved in launching a record label in 1978, the name Cherry Red stuck.

Punk band The Tights launched the label, and McNay, whose experience of record companies came from stints at Magnet and Bell/Arista, quickly added Morgan-Fisher and licensed US band Destroy All Monsters.

McNay's vision for Cherry Red was for a label that was 'as versatile as possible', capturing The Runaways for UK release, followed by emerging UK acts The Monochrome Set, Tracy Thorn and Ben Watt. Anagram Records was launched for The Vibrators and Angelic Upstarts, and El Records came and went before McNay took off in 1987 on a four-year tour of the world.

Returning to action in 1991, McNay set about acquiring rights to indie labels such as Flick Knife, Rondelet and Temple, and in 1995 he launched the celebrated *Football Collectors* series of songs from British football clubs.

Labels such as RPM, 7Ts, Analogue Baroque

CHERRY RED

and Sidewinder Sounds, alongside the re-launched Rev-Ola label, came under the Cherry Red banner to promote artists such as Bleach and Wakusei and catalogue releases from artists as diverse as Randy Edelman, The Dead Kennedys, Conway Twitty, Ivor Cutler and Marc Almond.

CHESS

THE WORLD'S MOST FAMOUS BLUES AND R&B LABEL WAS CREATED BY THE SONS OF POLISH IMMIGRANTS WHO ARRIVED IN AMERICA IN 1928. Leonard and Phil Chess settled in Chicago and became involved in managing taverns and clubs before they realised – in the words of Leonard's son, Marshall – that 'there was a market for race music'.

Aristocrat Records was their first music venture, established in 1947, featuring Muddy Waters and Sunnyland Slim. Three years later they re-named the label Chess Records – based on their Polish family name, Cryz – and set about leasing product from out-of-town producers, including Sun Records' founder Sam Phillips in Memphis.

Blues legends Howlin' Wolf, Jimmie Rodgers, Chuck Berry and Willie Dixon (who also acted as in-house producer, arranger and session player) were at the forefront of Chess' roster of artists. Their releases followed a progressive numerical sequence which began at 1425, the number of the Chess family home.

In order that the label could grow and succeed commercially, the staff at Chess had to forge relationships with America's important radio fraternity. Marshall Chess recounted to Joe Smith in *Off The Record* how it worked back in the '50s: 'Payola was how you got your records played. We would see a disc jockey and most of the time pay him off. It was how you did business.' Chess releases were licensed to Pye International for release in the UK, and artists like Chuck Berry, John Lee Hooker and Bo Diddley had a major impact on emerging British bands

No 1
Singles **1**
Albums -

No 1
Singles **1**
Albums -

CHESS

such as The Rolling stones, The Yardbirds and John Mayall's Bluesbreakers.

With the launch of subsidiary labels Checker (with signings Little Walter and Sonny Boy Williamson) and Argo (with jazz stars Ramsey Lewis and Wes Montgomery), Chess continued to expand until the Chess brothers switched their interest to radio stations in the early '60s, dropping most of the artists from their roster. Newer artists such as Koko Taylor, Fontella Bass and The Dells kept Chess in the charts, but after Leonard's death in 1969 the label was sold to the tape company GRT, and both Phil and his nephew Marshall left soon after. It was after this, in 1972, that Chess notched up their first and only Number One hit record, when Chuck Berry's 'My Ding-A-Ling' topped both the US and the UK singles charts.

The original Chess recordings survived various changes in ownership, including being acquired by Sugar Hill Records' founders Sylvia and Joe Robinson, before coming to rest with MCA in 1985, and they now form a valuable part of the Universal Music Group's catalogue. In 1999, many years after they left Chess, Marshall and his cousin Kevin Chess launched Cryz Records, using their original surname, and the label's first release was Murali Coryell's '2120', the address of the old Chess studios in Chicago.

No 1
Singles -
Albums -

No 1
Singles -
Albums **1**

CHINA

CHINA RECORDS WAS FOUNDED IN 1984 BY DEREK GREEN, WHO CHOSE THE NAME FOR HIS INDEPENDENT LABEL AFTER WITNESSING THE WELCOME GIVEN TO THE CHINESE TEAM AT THE 1984 OLYMPIC GAMES IN LOS ANGELES. 'As China was the buzzword of the '80s, there were always going to be lots of free headlines, and when people heard the word China they always thought in billions, so I decided it was going to be the name for my label,' said Green, who earlier spent ten years as managing director of A&M Records UK. The records released on the China label, continuing Green's fascination with things Chinese, carried the prefixes WOK for albums and WOL for singles, which produced wok 'n' wol as an eastern variation of a famous music genre.

Art Of Noise brought China its first success, and they later combined with rock legends Duane Eddy and Tom Jones to produce the hit singles 'Peter Gunn' and 'Kiss' respectively. Dogs D'Amour and The Levellers maintained China's profile in the '90s, when Morcheeba were added to the roster on the subsidiary Indochina label.

In 1998, China was acquired by Warner Music International, who had forged a marketing association with the independent in 1984, and the label was absorbed into Warner Music UK.

Chiswick

CHISWICK

ROGER ARMSTRONG AND EX-MANAGER OF THIN LIZZY TED CARROLL WERE PARTNERS IN A MARKET RECORD STALL WHEN THEY DECIDED TO LAUNCH CHISWICK RECORDS, which was named after an area of West London. Echoing the rock roots of '50s American rock labels, Chiswick signed Vince Taylor and Link Wray before moving into the burgeoning punk movement with bands such as The 101ers (an early Joe Strummer outfit) and Johnny And The Self Abusers. Motörhead launched their career with Chiswick, as did The Radio Stars, while Rocky Sharpe And The Replays, Sniff N The Tears and The Damned all produced chart singles for the EMI-distributed label.

Carroll and Armstrong moved on to create the Ace label as an offshoot of Chiswick in 1984. This new subsidiary enabled the duo to develop their 'hobby' of dealing in imported records on a formal basis.

When Chiswick was wound down (the final release came out in 1984), Ace unsurprisingly repackaged the label's finest titles while also dealing with re-issues from the original American Ace label. Over the years, Ace has obtained the UK rights to a succession of independent US labels, including Fantasy, Stax, Speciality and Vanguard.

CHRYSALIS

WHEN FORMER UNIVERSITY SOCIAL SECRETARIES CHRIS WRIGHT AND TERRY ELLIS DECIDED TO EMBARK ON A BUSINESS VENTURE TO FORM THEIR OWN RECORD COMPANY, they simply combined the names Chris and Ellis to form Chrysalis.

Ten Years After and Jethro Tull were both handled by Wright's and Ellis' original management company, and these bands formed the basis of a licensing deal with Island Records which led to the formation of Chrysalis in 1969. Under the deal, Island promised to reward the two young managers with their own label if they could notch up ten Top Ten albums or singles within three years. The target was achieved within a year, and so Chrysalis was formed, with its famous butterfly logo, and Tull and TYA were soon joined by Steeleye Span, Frankie Miller, Procol Harum and Leo Sayer.

One act that Chrysalis tried but failed to sign were The Sex Pistols, and Wright recalled this moment in his company's history: 'Malcolm McLaren said they were keen to sign with us but we were £10,000 short on the £50,000 they wanted. I called his bluff and they signed to EMI.' However, Generation X, Blondie, Nick Gilder and Billy Idol carried on the label's success story, which led ultimately to the opening of an American Chrysalis operation, replacing the company's initial US deal with Warner Bros Records, which had delivered US Number Ones for Leo Sayer.

The '80s brought the company more success with new romantic bands Ultravox and Spandau Ballet, along with US stars Debbie Harry, Pat Benatar and Huey Lewis And The News. However, despite the hits, Wright and Ellis were experiencing difficulties in their partnership. Wright once

No 1
Singles **10**
Albums **4**

No 1
Singles **17**
Albums **11**

CHRYSALIS

observed: 'The two or three years we had been fighting was not a good time for Chrysalis. By 1980 we were a much bigger company than Virgin, but by the time Terry and I split in 1985 they had sailed right past us.'

Wright added the MAM company and the independent label Ensign to the Chrysalis portfolio before EMI moved in with a $79 million bid for half of the company in 1989, when Sinéad O'Connor, World Party, The Proclaimers and Kenny Thomas (on the company's Cooltempo dance label) topped the roster. Within 18 months, EMI had exercised their option to acquire the remaining 50% of Chrysalis, and Wright had left the record label that he had founded two decades earlier, opting to focus on the Chrysalis Group

Meanwhile, the label went on to become a successful division of EMI UK, with Arrested Development (on Cooltempo) and the hugely successful Robbie Williams carrying on the name Chrysalis Records, which has merged with the existing EMI operation. Despite dropping Chrysalis from the name EMI:Chrysalis, the label's identity continues in the UK and the US, where it forms part of EMI's Virgin company.

No 1
Singles -
Albums -

No 1
Singles 1
Albums -

CHRYSALIS GROUP

FORMED BY ONE OF THE ORIGINAL FOUNDERS OF
CHRYSALIS RECORDS, Chris Wright's business empire
continued to enjoy the use of the name Chrysalis Group even
though EMI had acquired the use of the name Chrysalis as a
record label. Wright went on to launch a new involvement with
music, forming The Hit Label. Then, at the end of a two-year
exclusion period following the EMI deal struck in 1990 which
forbade him to form a contemporary rock/pop label, he set
up the Echo label with backing from Japanese company Pony
Canyon, rights owners in Asia. Echo's roster features Moloko
and Feeder.

Wright also backed the Papillon label, set up in 1999 and
featuring Jethro Tull (originally managed by Wright and his
then-partner Terry Ellis), Human League, Cliff Richard and
Deacon Blue, and the overseas Hit subsidiary, home to
catalogue material from Leo Sayer and the late Ian Dury.

US	UK
No 1	**No 1**
Singles **5**	Singles -
Albums **4**	Albums -

COLPIX/COLGEMS

COLUMBIA PICTURES INITIALLY USED THEIR COLPIX LABEL AS A VEHICLE TO RELEASE RECORDS THAT FEATURED IN THEIR FILM AND TELEVISION PRODUCTIONS, and the label reached the top of the charts in 1961 with The Marcels' version of Rodgers and Hart's standard 'Blue Moon', a song which appeared in at least four movies. A year later, actress Shelley Fabares recorded 'Johnny Angel' for Columbia TV's *The Donna Reed Show*, and also reached Number One on Colpix before Columbia's production company, Screen Gems, appeared in 1966 with the new record imprint Colgems and a ready-made pop act.

Screen Gems were responsible for making the TV series *The Monkees*, and the company decided to feature the successful group as recording stars on the Colgems subsidiary label. In a 13-month period, from November 1966, the group reached Number One in America three times with Colgems singles: 'Last Train To Clarksville', 'I'm A Believer' and 'Daydream Believer'.

Label executive Don Kirshner, who later created records for the non-existent group The Archies, recruited high-calibre songwriters such as Gerry Goffin, Carole King, Neil Sedaka and Neil Diamond to provide songs for The Monkees, whose records were released via RCA outside the US. The group – Michael Nesmith, Peter Tork, Davy Jones and Mickey Dolenz – didn't play on any of their early hits, but they were the only artists to chart on the Colgems label, alongside soundtracks from films such as *Casino Royale* and *Oliver!*.

COLUMBIA

COLUMBIA (CBS)

THE WORLD'S OLDEST AND PROBABLY MOST SUCCESSFUL RECORD COMPANY BEGAN LIFE NEARLY 115 YEARS AGO. Since 1887, as Columbia and CBS, the company has delivered best-sellers from artists ranging from blues star Bessie Smith and folk legend Bob Dylan to rock idol Bruce Springsteen and diva Mariah Carey.

The Columbia Phonograph Company was launched as on offshoot of the American Graphophone Company, which British inventors Chichester Bell (cousin of telephone inventor Alexander Graham Bell) and Charles Tainter had set up to develop a rival sound reproduction system to Thomas Edison's phonograph. The name Columbia arose when the company was formally incorporated as the Maryland, Delaware, and District Of Columbia franchise of the North American Graphophone Company.

While there was still considerable dispute about the technology involved in producing recorded music, in 1902 Columbia and Edison – who was now connected with the Victor company – agreed to standardise the production of 7" and 10" flat discs. The company expanded internationally, opening offices in Paris and London, but after the economic recession following the First World War Columbia was forced into receivership in 1923. Its British subsidiary was sold to local management, led by Managing Director Louis Sterling, who went on to expand the London-based Columbia International Company.

In 1926, Columbia acquired the leading blues label Okeh Records, which brought new jazz and blues musicians on board along with Bessie Smith, their own major signing. However, record sales fell dramatically during the American Depression, plummeting from 104 million in 1927 to around six million in 1932. Radio and refrigerator manufacturers Grigsby-Grunow, the new owners, went bankrupt in 1934 and sold the Columbia Phonograph Company to the American Record Corporation (ARC) for just $70,500, just nine years after the company had been bought for $2.5 million. ARC, owners of Brunswick and Vocalion, still struggled to make ends meet and soon the company was once again up for grabs.

The buyer this time was William S Paley, founder of the Columbia Broadcasting System, which was descended from the American radio network United Independent

COLUMBIA (CBS)

Broadcasters, part of the British-based Columbia operation. It was re-named Columbia Phonograph Broadcasting System before being shortened to CBS. Paley bought the whole ARC/Brunswick/Columbia operation in 1938 for $700,000, sold the early Brunswick and Vocalion material – along with the label names – to Decca US, and set about creating the CBS record empire. Success with big bands led by Count Basie, Duke Ellington and Benny Goodman re-established the Columbia name as part of CBS, and the arrival of crooner Frank Sinatra – who began his own CBS recording career in 1943 – brought the label a new focus of attention.

CBS engineers led by Dr Peter Goldmark invented the long-playing record in 1948 and determined the format for the recording of modern music for the next four decades, also enabling CBS to record America's major symphony orchestras and popular Broadway musicals.

The '50s saw CBS introduce the likes of Guy Mitchell, Frankie Laine and Johnny Ray, who appeared on the re-activated Okeh label. The label's strong MOR influences were still apparent in the early '60s in best-selling stars such as Doris Day, Johnny Mathis, Barbra Streisand and Andy Williams, whose album Days Of Wine And Roses had the honour of topping the first-ever Billboard Top 175 LP chart, combining mono and stereo releases in 1963.

However, in 1962 a veteran talent scout changed both the company's fortunes and its image. John Hammond began with ARC/Columbia, and with the signing of folk singer Bob Dylan he opened the doors of CBS to a new generation of rock/folk artists, including The Byrds and Simon And Garfunkel.

The arrival of a new company president, Clive Davis, also brought a new attitude towards pop music. 'Few of Columbia's A&R men lived in the world of the Top 40. The company's creative make-up was predominantly middle of the road. I sensed that Columbia had no choice but to change…or suffer.' Davis oversaw the signing of new American acts Blood, Sweat And Tears, Janis Joplin and Santana alongside Neil Diamond, UK stalwarts Pink Floyd (for America only) and a roster of country stars, including Johnny Cash, Marty Robbins and Tammy Wynette, while a deal with Gamble and Huff brought the Philly International label and soul music to Columbia.

COLUMBIA (CBS)

In the UK, the local CBS company set about signing hit acts, including chart-toppers Georgie Fame, The Tremeloes, Marmalade and David Essex.

In the mid '70s, CBS staff attorney Walter Yetnikoff was named president of CBS Records and he summed up the parent company's attitude to pop music thus: 'CBS has always been a broadcasting company first. They got interested in the record business when we started making lots of money but they never treated us with the same dignity as they did the broadcasting division.' However, Yetnikoff oversaw a further decade of growth, signing Bruce Springsteen, Billy Joel, Paul McCartney (for the US only), New Kids On The Block and Meat Loaf alongside UK signings Shakin' Stevens, Alison Moyet, Paul Young, Adam And The Ants and The Clash. CBS became the first record company to pass the magical $1 billion mark in sales.

In 1987, the Sony Music Entertainment Corporation acquired the CBS Records division from its parent company for $2 billion, and America's leading record company moved into Japanese ownership, along with all of its assorted label identities. As Sony didn't acquire the right to use the name CBS, they instead set about acquiring the outstanding rights to the Columbia label around the world from EMI. This enabled the new company to use the name Columbia as an international record brand. The honour of becoming the first Number One in the UK on the new Sony Columbia label fell to the Clash, with 'Should I Stay Or Should I Go?', and over the past ten years Mariah Carey, Michael Bolton, Will Smith and Ricky Martin have led the way for American musicians, alongside British successes Kula Shaker and The Manic Street Preachers and Australia's Savage Garden. The influential Loud label linked up with Columbia, following Sony's acquisition of the 50% holding in Loud previously held by BMG, and then merged with Relativity. Success post-2000 for the world's most senior record label came from veteran stars Bruce Springsteen and Barbra Streisand, alongside new signings Destiny's Child, A1, Spanish group Las Ketchup and, through Aware Records, John Mayer.

COLUMBIA (EMI)

FOR THREE YEARS, INTERNATIONAL DIVISIONS OF AMERICA'S COLUMBIA PHONOGRAPH COMPANY OPERATED IN FRANCE, GERMANY, POLAND AND RUSSIA BEFORE COLUMBIA'S EUROPEAN HEADQUARTERS WERE FINALLY ESTABLISHED IN LONDON IN 1900. While focusing mainly on American recordings, the Columbia catalogue also featured stars of British music hall, such as George Robey and Dan Leno, alongside a host of European classical celebrities. After the First World War, in order to maintain the considerable assets of the European business, a British registered company was formed as the Columbia Graphophone Company Limited, although all assets and share capital remained with the American parent company.

However, with the American company in serious financial trouble and heading for receivership, the British division was acquired by a new board led by Managing Director Louis Sterling. The resulting British company, which in 1929 boasted profits of £500,000, expanded by acquiring the Okeh label for the UK and United Independent Broadcasters radio network (a forerunner of the mighty CBS corporation) from America, along with Carl Lindstrom's Dutch/German Transoceanic Trading, which included the Parlophone and Odeon labels, the successful Japanese company Nipponphone and the recording division of France's prestigious Pathé company.

Throughout the '20s, Columbia boasted big bands, recordings from hit shows and major classical recordings in their catalogue, alongside the legendary 1926 recording of 'The Laughing Policeman' by Charles Penrose. However, the onset of the Depression of the '30s brought about a move that led to the creation of the world's greatest record company. In June 1939 Columbia merged its interests with its great rival, the Gramophone Company, to form Electric And Musical Industries, which were known thereafter as EMI.

As part of the new EMI company, Columbia took its place alongside the established HMV and developing Parlophone labels, and focused on classical recordings, issuing releases by such great names as Tito Gobi, Kathleen Ferrier and Maria Callas. In the '50s, when EMI lost its distribution deals with American giants RCA and CBS, it

No 1
Singles -
Albums -

No 1
Singles **50**
Albums **5**

COLUMBIA (EMI)

was forced to search out new British talent, and Columbia was on its way to enjoying two decades as one of the UK's most successful pop labels. Ruby Murray, Eddie Calvert and Russ Conway were followed by new British rock/pop stars Cliff Richard, The Shadows and Helen Shapiro, all of whom were produced by staff producer Norrie Paramor.

The '60s beat boom brought more talent to Columbia, with Gerry And The Pacemakers (the only act from Brian Epstein's Liverpool stable not to appear on the Parlophone label), The Animals, The Dave Clark Five, Herman's Hermits and (initially) Pink Floyd all helping to build Columbia's stature in the UK.

EMI launched their EMI label in 1972, and former Columbia stalwarts such as Cliff Richard and The Shadows soon switched to the new imprint, thereby ending Columbia's reign as a chart-topping pop label. For a further decade, Columbia was used as a secondary classical label behind HMV, until EMI – seeking to end the issue with CBS relating to global ownership of the Columbia name – resorted to placing an advertisement in the music trade magazine *Billboard* offering the sale of an unnamed label.

While nothing came of the advert, Sony's purchase of the CBS Records division (although not the CBS imprint) in 1987 heightened the need for the new Japanese owners to find a replacement for the CBS label, which had been used instead of Columbia outside the US. A deal was eventually struck at the turn of the '90s, and, after 70 years, EMI finally sold Sony the rights to the Columbia name in the UK and in other assorted international territories.

CONCORD RECORDS

CONCORD

CONCORD RECORDS WAS ESTABLISHED IN 1973 BY CONCORD JAZZ FESTIVAL ORGANISER CARL JEFFERSON, and was home to jazz greats such as Stan Getz, Mel Torme, Gary Burton and Joe Pass.

Over the years, Concord continued to represent the world's leading jazz artists under the watchful eye of Jefferson, who died in 1995. A year before his death, Jefferson sold the company to Alliance Entertainment and Concord linked with labels such as Stretch, Peak, Feinery and the Playboy Jazz label.

In 1999, Concord came under new ownership when Norman Lear and Hal Gaba acquired the label after Alliance hit financial difficulties and, from their Los Angeles base, have added artists such as Barry Manilow, Peter Cincotti and Ray Charles.

CONTEMPORARY

CONTEMPORARY

THE MODERN JAZZ LABEL CONTEMPORARY WAS LAUNCHED IN 1951 BY LESTER KOENIG, FOUNDER OF THE GOOD TIME TRADITIONAL JAZZ LABEL. THE LOS-ANGELES-BASED LABEL, which became a pioneer in high-quality pressings packaged with stunning graphic designs, released the first stereo jazz records in 1956, capturing the finest West Coast jazzers, such as Shelly Mann, Art Pepper and Hampton Hawes, alongside the East Coast giants Sonny Rollins and Ornette Coleman. Koenig died in 1977, and in 1984 Contemporary was acquired by Fantasy, Inc, who added the likes of Terry Gibbs, Buddy de Franco and Carol Sloane to the roster.

COOKING VINYL

LAUNCHED IN THE UK IN 1986, Cooking Vinyl sprang to prominence through artists such as Michelle Shocked (whose album *Texas Campfire Tapes*, produced by the label's original A&R executive, Peter Lawrence, was among its first releases), Bert Jansch and Billy Bragg.

Newer additions to the London-based independent label include Richard Thompson, Ian McCulloch, Bob Mould, Canadian Bruce Cockburn and, from America, The Minus 5, which boasts REM's Peter Buck as an occasional member, plus Ryan Adams' début recording.

Cooking Vinyl, who are represented internationally through a network of licence deals, signed with Spinart in America in 2001 and, a year later, linked with US label Tone-Cool Records to release their recordings outside America.

No 1
Singles **1**
Albums -

No 1
Singles **4**
Albums -

CORAL

ESTABLISHED AS A SUBSIDIARY OF DECCA US, Coral Records existed for a little under two decades but is best remembered for releasing the records made by Buddy Holly And The Crickets between 1957 and 1959.

After its creation in 1949, Coral brought The McGuire Sisters, Teresa Brewer and Debbie Reynolds (the label's only US Number One artist and mother of Carrie Fisher, who starred as Princess Leia in the *Stars Wars* trilogy) to the fore, although their releases appeared in the UK on Decca's Vogue-Coral imprint.

Before merging with Brunswick (which had been bought by Decca in 1942), Coral dabbled in rock 'n' roll with Johnny Burnette, but the newly-created combined label delivered Texan singer Buddy Holly and his group, The Crickets, in 1957. While Holly was actually signed to Coral, and The Crickets to Brunswick, the records featured all the same artists and in the UK were all released on Coral. After Holly's death in a plane crash in 1959 (after he and the group had split a year earlier), The Crickets departed to join Liberty's roster. The label continued, releasing the music of soul singer Jackie Wilson along with Holly's demos and catalogue items, but it was on its last legs. When Decca US was bought by MCA in 1962, they closed down Coral very soon afterwards. Paul McCartney maintained an interest in Buddy Holly And The Crickets material released by Coral/Brunswick by staging tribute concerts following his 1976 purchase of the publishing rights to Holly's compositions.

No 1
Singles -
Albums -

No 1
Singles **4**
Albums **4**

CREATION

SCOTTISH FORMER BRITISH RAIL CLERK ALAN McGEE MOVED TO LONDON IN 1982 AND LAUNCHED A 'MOVEABLE VENUE' CALLED THE LIVING ROOM, in partnership with Dick Green. A year later, he formed Creation Records

Fellow Scots The Jesus And Mary Chain – who were managed by McGee – were the label's first major signings, joining the label on the back of a series of low-budget, limited-edition single releases. McGee used Creation (named after an obscure '60s band) to release psychedelic and punk records by the likes of The Pastels, Primal Scream, My Bloody Valentine, House Of Love and McGee's own band, Biff Bang Pow.

In the '90s, McGee saw the need to settle Creation's financial positions, which he did by selling 49% of his label to the giant Sony Corporation for a reported £3 million. Now financially solvent, McGee and Creation proceeded to attract The Boo Radleys, Ride and Teenage Fanclub, although they finally hit the big time with Manchester group Oasis, whose chart domination between 1994 and 1997 made McGee and his label the favourite pop interest of the media…and some politicians! McGee emphasised his a close involvement in his label's A&R policy by explaining that 'the criteria for signing a group is if I like them'.

The oddball Creation subsidiary Rev-ola gave the world William 'Captain Kirk' Shatner's spoken-word recordings, alongside poet Ivor Cutler and cult band Jonathan Richman And The Modern Lovers.

Creation existed successfully for over 15 years, boasting the likes of Kevin Rowland, Ruby, St Etienne, Super Furry Animals and Bernard Butler on its roster, and according to McGee the label deserved more credit than it was given. 'I don't feel enough people recognise what a great British label Creation is.'

At the end of 1999, McGee shocked the music industry by announcing his decision to leave Creation in order to focus his attention on new business areas involving the internet, and to work on his radio and film interests. The label identity disappeared in early 2000 with Primal Scream's *Xtrmntr* album and, while big-hitters Oasis switched to their own Big Brother imprint, McGee set up a new multimedia company: Poptones.

No 1
Singles **5**
Albums **4**

No 1
Singles **1**
Albums -

CURB

MIKE CURB, A CALIFORNIAN JINGLE-WRITER TURNED SONGWRITER AND PRODUCER, WAS RESPONSIBLE FOR SIGNING THE MULTI-MILLION-SELLING OSMONDS TO MGM DURING HIS TIME AS THE LABEL'S PRESIDENT, during which time he also formed and recorded his own choir, The Mike Curb Congregation. Curb started his eponymous record label after leaving MGM in 1973, also forming Curb Productions. The company linked up with Warner Bros Records to release US Number One singles by Shaun Cassidy (brother of David), Debby Boone (daughter of Pat), The Bellamy Brothers and Exile. At various times, Curb linked his company with RCA, Capitol and MCA in order to release records by country acts such as The Judds and Sawyer Brown. He later went on to pursue a political career, which resulted in him being elected lieutenant-governor of California in 1978.

In addition to handling The Osmonds' and The Four Seasons' catalogues, his revamped Curb label hit the big time in the late '90s with a new breed of country artists, including LeAnn Rimes (whose total sales now exceed 20 million albums), Tim McGraw, Jo Dee Messina and Lyle Lovett, who is the only artist linked with a joint venture between Curb and MCA.

The label reportedly held an impressive 15% share of America's country-music market, and has forged an ongoing manufacturing, distribution and licensing agreement with Warner Music Group, who made the Asylum name available to Curb.

RECORDS ®

No 1
Singles **1**
Albums **1**

No 1
Singles -
Albums -

CURTOM

SWEET SOUL SINGER CURTIS MAYFIELD LAUNCHED CURTOM RECORDS IN 1968 AFTER A TEN-YEAR CAREER WITH THE CHICAGO-BASED SINGING GROUP THE IMPRESSIONS. Through his standing as a singer, writer and producer in Chicago, he worked with Jerry Butler, Major Lance and Gene Chandler, and both Chandler and The Impressions (minus Mayfield) recorded for Curtom, and their music was released alongside the label owner's solo recordings.

The label enjoyed major chart success with The Staple Singers' 'Let's Do It Again' in 1975, which was written and produced by Mayfield, but as disco and funk became more popular so Curtom's soul releases declined in popularity and Curtom Records closed in 1980.

Mayfield went on to release 'Something To Believe In' with a Curtom imprint in 1989, but in the following year he became paralysed from the neck down after an accident onstage. He died in December 1999.

CASH MONEY – see Universal

CASTLE – see Sanctuary

CGD – see Sugar

CHART – see TK

CHECKER – see Chess

CMC – see Sanctuary

COOLTEMPO – see Chrysalis/EMI

COTILLION – see Atlantic

CREATION – see Polydor/RSO

CROWN – see Modern

CRYZ – see Chess

CUB – see MGM

DARK HORSE

AFTER THE PROBLEMS THAT THE BEATLES ENCOUNTERED AT APPLE, George Harrison was the first member of the band to venture back into the record business in a solo capacity, founding his own Dark Horse label in the mid '70s. Home to Harrison's own recordings (although he was still technically signed to EMI), Dark Horse's only major chart success came with the duo Splinter, who in 1974 had a Top 20 hit with 'Costafine Town'. The label continued to thrive throughout the '80s after Harrison left EMI and signed to Warner Bros Records, while his solo albums continued to carry the Dark Horse logo, which also appeared on his final album, Brainwashed, issued on Parlophone through EMI.

No 1
Singles **1**
Albums **6**

No 1
Singles -
Albums -

DEATH ROW

RAP MUSIC'S MIGHTIEST LABEL, DEATH ROW, SOLD OVER 18 MILLION RECORDS IN ITS FIRST FOUR YEARS AFTER BEING SET UP IN LOS ANGELES IN 1992 BY MARION 'SUGE' KNIGHT, who vowed that his record company would become the Motown of the '90s and asserted that he was a latter-day Berry Gordy.

Knight began his career in the music business with his Funky Enough label, which featured Vanilla Ice, and he then launched Futureshock Records, which became Death Row after Knight persuaded Dr Dre to leave NWA and form the company, using the name of a label originally formed by LA couple Michael and Lydia Harris.

With record producer Jimmy Iovine providing $10 million in financial support for the label, and also distributing the records through his Interscope company, Death Row hit the jackpot with its first three albums from Dr Dre, Snoop Doggy Dogg and the soundtrack to the movie *Above The Rim*, all of which became multi-platinum sellers. Despite the hits, however, America's anti-rap movement successfully forced the giant US corporation Time Warner to end its association with Interscope and Death Row in 1990.

New signing 2Pac Shakur acknowledged the contribution of Dre, Snoop and others, but claimed: 'I'm gonna take Death Row to the next level.' After linking with Universal, again through Interscope, Death Row entered into a bitter feud with fellow rapper and entrepreneur Sean Combs and his New York-based Bad Boy label. It has been claimed that the war – part of a supposed East/West Coast rivalry – resulted in the murders of Death Row's Shakur and Bad Boy's Notorious BIG.

In the midst of this non-music activity, Dr Dre left Death Row, Snoop sued the label and in 1997 founder Knight was sentenced to nine years in prison. With no new major artists, Death Row relied on the release of compilation albums to keep its name alive, including the release of Greatest Hits packages of past label successes.

DECCA

DECCA

A LEADING BRITISH RECORD COMPANY FOR OVER 50 YEARS, DECCA WAS ONE OF THE FIRST UK MUSIC COMPANIES TO ESTABLISH AN AMERICAN SUBSIDIARY AND SET ITS SIGHTS ON THE IMPORTANT US RECORD MARKET.

British stockbroker Sir Edward Lewis acquired the Decca Gramophone Company in 1929 and launched Decca Records in the same year. The label's first success came with '30s big band leaders Ambrose and Jack Hylton, and this was followed by the acquisition of American stars Bing Crosby and Al Jolson through the purchase of the British arm of Brunswick. In order to make an impression in the American record business, Lewis set up American Decca in 1934, under the leadership of former Brunswick head Jack Kapp, who added to the label an array of major stars, such as The Mills Brothers, Louis Armstrong, The Ink Spots, Ella Fitzgerald and Bing Crosby, whose recording of 'White Christmas' has sold over 30 million copies since 1942.

After MCA's acquisition of Decca US, Lewis created London Records as his new American company in 1947, which was originally intended to operate alongside Decca UK. This label can lay claim to being the first to have British artists topping both the American singles and albums charts, with Vera Lynn ('Auf Wiederseh'n' in 1952) and Mantovani (Music Of Victor Herbert in 1953).

In America, Decca US's chart-topping acts such as Bill Haley and Brenda Lee appeared on MCA's Decca imprint, while in the UK they appeared on the Brunswick label because the British company retained rights to American recordings until the mid '70s.

London and Decca together set about launching a host of new pop stars, such as Teresa Brewer, Lonnie Donegan, Tommy Steele and Billy Fury. The Tornados' 'Telstar' was a massive international hit in 1962, and the label followed this success by signing new acts such as The Rolling Stones, Brian Poole And The Tremeloes, The Bachelors, The Moody Blues, Tom Jones and Engelbert Humperdinck. (Legend has it that one major Merseybeat group managed to get away from Decca when A&R man Dick Rowe famously turned down The Beatles in order to sign Brian Poole.)

No 1
Singles **5**
Albums **5**

No 1
Singles **37**
Albums **15**

DECCA

During Decca's golden period of signing British pop talent, London Records leased repertoire for UK release from a host of small American labels who represented artists such as Little Richard, The Everly Brothers, Del Shannon, Roy Orbison, The Crystals and The Ronettes, and this helped to maintain Decca's position as a world-class operation. The company's classical recordings – led by Sir George Solti – were an immensely successful part of Decca's operation, and this was due in part to the high-quality reproduction of the recordings, thanks to their FFRR (Full Frequency Range Recordings) technique.

From the Second World War onwards, Decca UK also established itself as a leading radar and electronics company along with its more familiar music operations, but its international music business lagged behind that of their great rivals, EMI. During the '70s, when acts like The Rolling Stones defected and the US labels that came through London began to set up their own operations, Decca's fortunes faded. Finally, after Sir Edward Lewis' death in 1980, Polygram acquired what was left of Decca and re-introduced the London label worldwide for the release of pop repertoire, as the Decca name was owned by MCA in the US. Following Universal's acquisition of MCA, and ultimately of Polygram in 1998, all of the original Decca/London recordings and labels were again housed under one roof.

In 1999, Decca was merged with the Philips Music Group, a division of Universal Classics And Jazz, releasing music by star names such as Luciano Pavarotti, Vladimir Ashkenazy and Sarah Brightman.

No 1
Singles -
Albums -

No 1
Singles -
Albums 1

DECONSTRUCTION

THE BRITISH INDEPENDENT LABEL Deconstruction was founded in 1987, and its aim was to reflect and promote interest in the UK's rapidly-emerging dance music business.

Pete Hadfield and Keith Blackhurst worked in various areas of the music business before getting together to form Deconstruction. Early releases came from T-Coy and Richie Close, but it was Italian dance act Black Box's massive 1988 hit 'Ride On Time' that consolidated the label's reputation.

After seven years as an independent company, Deconstruction linked with BMG and delivered million-sellers M People to the major label. Expanding within BMG, Deconstruction released music by hit acts such as Kylie Minogue, Republica, Beth Orton and Robert Miles, before the label became a wholly-owned subsidiary of BMG in 1998.

No 1
Singles **4**
Albums **15**

No 1
Singles -
Albums -

DEF JAM

THE WORLD'S MOST INFLUENTIAL (and arguably most profitable) rap label came into being in New York in 1984 when white college student Rick Rubin paired up with black entreprenuer Russell Simmons, brother of Run DMC's Joseph Simmons. Rubin had actually launched the label while still at New York University, after his friendship with DJ Jazz Jay had introduced him to the city's emerging club music. A meeting with Simmons – already a producer and manager of The Beastie Boys and Run-DMC through his own Rush Artists company – took Def Jam to the next level.

Sharing an initial investment of $8,000, Rubin and Simmons launched the label with LL Cool J, and within a year Def Jam had signed a marketing and promotion deal with CBS. Public Enemy and The Beastie Boys – whose album *Licensed To III* became the biggest-selling rap album of the time – joined LL Cool J in making the label a flagship for rap music.

After working together for only four years, Rubin and Simmons began to grow apart, and Rubin eventually took his share of the company to Los Angeles, where he created Def American Records. Meanwhile, in 1990 Simmons re-negotiated the deal with Sony (now the new owners of CBS) to launch RAL (Rush Associated Labels), which would include the Def Jam label. The deal was reported to be the music industry's largest-ever subsidiary deal, with Def Jam receiving $3 million a year to cover operating costs.

Alongside new acts Foxy Brown and Method Man, LL Cool J kept Def Jam in the spotlight through the mid '90s, and eventually Polygram Music acquired a 60% stake in the company. Following Universal Music's take over of Polygram in 1998, Def Jam – with its sister imprints Ruff Ryders and Def Soul – was placed alongside the Island and Mercury labels under the banner IDJMG (Island/Def Jam/Mercury Group), but continued to produce chart-topping artists such as Ja Rule, Ashanti and Jay-2.

DEMON

DEMON

WHEN JAKE RIVERA FOUNDED DEMON RECORDS WITH ANDREW LAUDER IN 1980, HE SET SOMETHING OF A WORLD RECORD, as it was the fourth record label that he had launched in just over three years. The first label he founded was Stiff in 1977, after which he moved on to form Radar in 1978, which was closely followed by F-Beat and finally Demon Records, whose early singles-only releases featured records by The Subterraneans and Department S, whose song 'Is Vic There?' was the label's first chart hit. Major album artists later emerged to give Demon Records a level of credibility, including former Stiff and Radar acts Elvis Costello and Nick Lowe, along with American blues star Robert Cray. The label then introduced the re-issue subsidiary Edsel, and also linked with other companies, such as American soul label Hi Records while also launching the careers of The Shamen, Paul Brady and Christy Moore.

In 1998, Demon was acquired by a subsidiary of the UK retail giant Kingfisher, owners of Woolworths, and a year later was merged with the Kingfisher-owned budget label Westside as part of the parent company's VCI audio operation.

No 1
Singles -
Albums -

No 1
Singles 1
Albums -

DERAM

WHILE DERAM WAS SET UP BY DECCA UK AS A LABEL FOR ALTERNATIVE ARTISTS, it never really competed with the more progressive/underground Harvest and Vertigo imprints launched in 1969 by EMI and Philips respectively. The label first saw the light of day in 1966 with Cat Stevens, and he was quickly followed by the signing of two acts from Denny Cordell's production company, The Move and Procol Harum, whose 'Whiter Shade Of Pale' was their only Deram release and the label's only Number One hit.

Deram's impressive track record between 1967 and 1970 resulted in the emergence of hit acts such as The Moody Blues (originally signed to Decca in 1964, before switching to Deram in 1967 and releasing records on their own Threshold imprint three years later), Amen Corner, The Flowerpot Men, Whistling Jack Smith, The Honey Bus, Brotherhood Of Man and White Plains.

By the early '70s, Deram was again playing second fiddle to Decca, and hits by East Of Eden and, finally, ex-Marmalade singer Junior Campbell in 1973 were Deram's last successes before it disappeared into the vaults.

DG

FOUNDED OVER A CENTURY AGO, DEUTSCHE GRAMMOPHON CAN TRACE ITS ORIGINS TO EMILE BERLINER, the inventor of the gramophone and the gramophone record, who established DG in 1898 on his return to his native Hanover from America, only a year after the British Gramophone company was established. Berliner's grandson Oliver believes that the DG record company had a very special place in his grandfather's heart. 'Perhaps it was because his brother ran the company, or because it was located in his hometown, or because it was where DG pressed the first records in Europe.'

Opera stars Chaliapin and Caruso recorded for DG in the early years of the 20th century, and in 1916 the company experienced a split between the original German and British Gramophone companies. In 1917, Polyphon-Musikwerke of Leipzig acquired the German arm of DG, which led to the creation of the Polydor label in 1924. Liquidation and restructuring brought about a new Deutsche Grammophon Gmbh in 1937, and the famous German conductor Herbert von Karajan made his début for the label in that year. The Siemens company became the sole owners of the firm in 1941, but shortly afterwards the factory, the offices and the studios were all destroyed by bombs in the Second World War.

In 1949, after the EMI company Electrola began to use the HMV label, DG – whose original British links had previously allowed them to use the dog and trumpet logo – launched their now famous yellow label, which features a tulip crown.

The merger of Siemens and the music arm of Dutch electronics giant Philips in 1962 led to the formation of a combined DG/Philips company which included the Archiv label. Major conductors and soloists – such as Leonard Bernstein, Dietrich Fischer-Dieskau, Anne Sophie Mutter, Bryn Terfel, The Amadeus Quartet and Andre Previn – flocked to DG, enhancing its reputation as the world's leading classical label.

As a division of the Polygram music operation, which was acquired by Seagrams Universal Music Group in 1998, DG celebrated 100 years in the business by becoming part of the world's largest music company.

No 1
Singles -
Albums -

No 1
Singles -
Albums **4**

DJM

SINGER, SONGWRITER AND MUSIC PUBLISHER
DICK JAMES LITERALLY SOLD THE BEATLES AND
USED THE PROCEEDS TO START DJM RECORDS IN
1969. Responsible for writing Max Bygraves' children's
favourite 'You're A Pink Toothbrush, I'm A Blue Toothbrush',
James was signed to Parlophone by producer George Martin,
and together they wrote and recorded the famous theme of
the '50s TV series *Robin Hood*.

After moving into music publishing, James was introduced
to The Beatles by Martin and his Northern Songs company
successfully published the famous Lennon and McCartney
compositions. James launched DJM after the sale of Northern
Songs, and after dissolving his partnership with Larry Page
and Page One Records, home to the legendary Troggs. DJM's
limited roster included comedian Jasper Carrott (who charted
with a dubious version of 'The Magic Roundabout') and singer
Elton John, who was also published by James, together with
co-writer Bernie Taupin. However, the label's biggest hit came
with Mr Bloe's 1970 Number Two 'Groovin' With Mr Bloe'.

In 1973, Elton John left the label and his subsequent
acrimonious lawsuit against DJM over royalty payments
contributed hugely to the label's downfall. The DJM catalogue
was acquired by Polygram after Dick James' death in 1986.

No 1
Singles **7**
Albums **2**

No 1
Singles -
Albums -

DOT

RECORD STORE OWNER RANDY WOOD SET UP DOT RECORDS IN GALLATIN, TEXAS, IN 1951. After early R&B releases, including those by Arthur Alexander, within five years it became a major pop label.

Dot's status came about thanks to actor-turned-singer Tab Hunter and teen sensation Pat Boone, who – despite some criticism of his pop covers of soul and R&B originals – notched up more than a dozen million-selling singles for the label in under a decade. Part of Dot's success was due to Wood's introduction of the automatic shipping of records which he thought were hits to distributors in consignments of over 200,000. Even though he was prepared to take back unsold product, distributors balked at paying for the whole order, and so Wood initiated the concept of dated 30-, 60- or 90-day billing.

Wood moved Dot from Texas to Hollywood in 1956, and by licensing releases from other labels the company enjoyed a series of surf hits from The Surfaris, The Chantays and The Rumblers. Jimmy Gilmer's 1963 hit 'Sugar Shack' was the last genuine Number One release by Dot US before Wood sold the label to Gulf And Western in 1965, where it became part of the ABC Group and boasted Freddy Fender on ABC/Dot.

Wood re-appeared in 1967 as a partner in the Ranwood Record Company (which was named after him), alongside bandleader's son Larry Wells and Ranwood act Lawrence Welk, who ultimately joined the Wells Music Group when they acquired Ranwood in 1979.

No 1
Singles -
Albums **2**

No 1
Singles -
Albums -

DREAMWORKS

WHEN DAVID GEFFEN LEFT THE GEFFEN RECORDS COMPANY THAT HE HAD PREVIOUSLY SOLD TO MCA IN 1995, he teamed up with two of America's most successful entertainment moguls: film producer Steven Spielberg and former Disney executive Jeffrey Katzenberg. Together they created DreamWorks SKG, which included a newly-created record label alongside the film and television companies. With former Warner Bros Records boss Mo Ostin at the helm, DreamWorks quickly offered George Michael a new American home after his unsuccessful lawsuit against Sony left him without a record label. They released his album *Older* in 1996.

Former Warner Bros stalwart Randy Newman followed Ostin to DreamWorks, where he joined chart acts eels, Morphine, Toby Keith and Powerman 5000 on the roster, which also featured new addition Tamar Braxton, sister of million-selling artist Toni Braxton and Nelly Furtado. In 2003, Dreamworks linked with former Priority Records founder Bryan Turner's Melee Entertainment and secured a Number One album for veteran soul act The Isley Brothers.

No 1
Singles **5**
Albums **1**

No 1
Singles -
Albums -

DUNHILL

LOU ADLER'S COMPANY DUNHILL PRODUCTIONS, launched in 1964, was engaged in numerous production and songwriting ventures before the company was transformed into Dunhill Records in 1965.

Barry McGuire was responsible for the label's first US Number One, and also for introducing hit makers The Mamas And The Papas to Adler and his new label. While Richard Harris and The Grassroots continued to deliver hits for Dunhill, Adler carried on with his outside production work with the likes of Jan And Dean and Johnny Rivers.

In 1966 Adler sold the Dunhill label to distributors ABC, and before launching his follow-up label in 1967, Ode Records, Adler joined up with four colleagues to help sponsor and organise the legendary Monterey Pop Festival.

DANCING CAT – see Windham Hill

DATA – see Ministry Of Sound

DAWN – see Pye

DEDICATED – see Arista

DEF AMERICA – see American Recordings

DEFECTED – see Ministry Of Sound

DEF SOUL – see Def Jam

DELUXE – see King

DISA – see Univision

DISCOVERY – see Elektra

DR JAZZ – see Fantasy

DUCK – see Reprise

EAGLE ROCK
ENTERTAINMENT LIMITED

EAGLE ROCK

FORMED IN 1997 BY TERRY SHAND, founder of the
Castle catalogue company, Eagle Rock includes record labels,
video production and TV programming.

The company's Eagle Records label boasts recordings
from artists such as Joe Cocker, Simple Minds, John Mayall,
Bob Geldof and Alan Parsons and has offices in France,
Germany, Italy and Spain, while sister label Spitfire Records
was formed in America in 1999 and operated as a hard-
rock/metal imprint representing Alice Cooper and Deep Purple
plus Black Label Society and Testament.

No 1
Singles **1**
Albums **1**

No 1
Singles **5**
Albums **9**

EASTWEST

THE EASTWEST LABEL, WHICH CURRENTLY BOASTS THE LIKES OF SIMPLY RED AND CHRIS REA, first appeared in 1955 as a subsidiary of Atlantic intended to release recordings made by producers Lee Hazlewood and Lester Sill. While the label's name signified the two coasts of America, East actually referred to New York and West to Phoenix.

The Kingsmen's 'Weekend' was the only hit put out by EastWest before the label went into hibernation, to be re-activated in 1989 by Nesuhi Ertegun, brother of Atlantic Records founder Ahmet. After retiring from his post as head of the WEA International division of the Warner Music Group, Ertegun set up EastWest as a label to represent the company's jazz catalogue and new jazz signings. Unfortunately, Ertegun died before the label got under way. EastWest America was then set up as part of Atlantic, while Warner Music International used the EastWest name as a source of local repertoire in Australia, Brazil France, Germany, Italy, Japan, Spain and the UK.

EastWest America hit the big time with Snow in 1993, and ultimately became a division of the Elektra Entertainment company. Meanwhile, EastWest UK delivered the million-selling singer/songwriter David Gray and also adopted Mushroom Records UK, following its acquisition by Warner Music UK.

EDEL

FORMED IN GERMANY IN 1986 AS A COMPANY SELLING SOUNDTRACKS BY MAIL ORDER, within a decade Edel became one of Europe's largest and most important independent record companies, boasting operations in Austria, Benelux, Italy, Scandinavia, Spain and the UK. Founder Michael Haentjes launched Edel's first domestic A&R operation in 1992 and quickly added a classical arm before launching his European affiliates in 1995. Artists such as Aaron Carter, Jennifer Paige, Holly Johnson, Tony di Bart, Sash! and Scooter established Edel as a successful pop music label, and the company was floated on the Frankfurt Stock Exchange in 1998.

Joint European ventures with UK companies Mute and Beggars Banquet, European licensing deals with US companies such as Disney, the acquisition of a majority share of the Eagle Rock company in Britain, the purchase of Belgium's pan-European indie act Play It Again Sam and the formation of an American label helped to establish Hamburg-based Edel as a major international music company. However, following restructuring, Edel downscaled its international operations, lost a number of licensing deals and sold its stake in the German TV station Viva, but still managed to hang on to its position as Germany's biggest independent.

ELEKTRA

JAC HOLZMAN WAS A STUDENT IN ANNAPOLIS, MARYLAND, WHEN HE FOUNDED ELEKTRA RECORDS IN 1950 WITH $300 OF HIS OWN MONEY, given to him for his bar mitzvah, and an equal amount invested by fellow student and partner Paul Rickholt. The label began life by issuing *New Songs* by Georgianna Bannister and John Gruen as EKLP1 in 1952.

Holzman, whose early interest lay in original American music, says that he named his label after the Greek demi-goddess Electra, who presided over the artistic muses, but changed one letter. In his biography *Follow The Muse*, he explains: 'Electra with a C struck me as too soft, and I had always admired the use of Ks by Kodak, and I turned two Ms on their side to create a distinctive E for the label.'

The first Elektra offices were in a storefront in Greenwich Village, New York, and in its early days Holzman combined his twin loves of music and engineering by producing his own records. He claims that none of his early albums cost more than $45 to make. The company then moved to larger offices in nearby Bleecker Street, Holzman bought out his friend's original investment in 1954, and Elektra moved into a more commercial sphere, releasing music from Josh White, and New York's finest contemporary folk stars – Judy Collins, Tom Paxton, Fred Neil and Phil Ochs – were on board soon afterwards.

Electric rock was the next genre for Elektra, with Paul Butterfield, Love and The Doors heading the roster. Holzman's deal with The Doors involved Elektra paying all recording costs plus $5,000 in cash against a 5% royalty with a commitment for three albums. He later described it as 'slightly on the generous side of a standard deal in 1966'.

Bread, Tom Rush, Carly Simon, MC5 and The Incredible String Band took Elektra into the next stage of its life as part of the giant Warner Communications company, which involved a redesigned logo featuring a giant E with, in some cases, a caterpillar or a butterfly. Holzman sold his label in 1970 for $10 million but remained at its head for another three years, until David Geffen – whose Asylum label had become part of Warner Communications in 1972 – was put in charge of a new combined

No 1	No 1
Singles **13**	Singles -
Albums **10**	Albums **5**

ELEKTRA

Elektra/Asylum label. Geffen's view of the merger was simple: 'The success rate at Asylum was higher than any other record company in history, and putting the two companies together revitalised Elektra big time.' At this point, Holzman departed to become chief technologist for Warner and continued to work in communications and media before launching the Discovery label, which ultimately became part of the Warner Music Group. Asylum's roster of stars included Jackson Browne, The Eagles and Joni Mitchell, and the new joint company became the E in Warner Communications' WEA division, along with Warner Bros Records and Atlantic.

After Geffen departed in the mid '70s, Elektra set about creating a new roster of artists, adding The Cars, Mötley Crüe, Anita Baker, Metallica and Tracy Chapman to their books, along with UK groups Queen, Simply Red and The Cure, who found an American home in the new, expanded Elektra Entertainment company, with its modern logo of a pair of balancing Es (above). Acts such as En Vogue, AC/DC, Phish, Third Eye Blind and Linda Ronstadt, alongside hit makers Missy Elliott, Staind and Lil' Mo have maintained the label's reputation for musical diversification.

Nearly 50 years after Holzman set the label rolling in 'the Village', Elektra remains in New York City and current chairman/CEO Sylvia Rhone believes that the label reflects the spirit and musical diversity of the city. 'From the folk revival of the '60s to the hip-hop explosion of the '90s, Elektra has been there.'

EMI Records

EMI

DESPITE THE FACT THAT THE EMI COMPANY WAS
ACTUALLY FOUNDED IN 1931, it was another 40 years
before the EMI label was created, with T Rex's 1972 release
'Metal Guru' the first hit on the new imprint.

When the EMI company re-assigned HMV as a classical
label and were unable to solve the problems arising from
having to share the rights to the Columbia name with CBS,
they introduced EMI as a pop label, alongside Parlophone
and Harvest. Pilot, Steve Harley And Cockney Rebel and
Queen were among the first acts signed to EMI, while former
Columbia stalwarts Cliff Richard and The Shadows transferred
to the label.

In America, Capitol Records used the EMI label to release
records by acts signed to their sister companies around the
world, including The Hollies and EMI Sweden's Blue Swede,
who topped the US charts with 'Hooked On A Feeling' in 1974.

A roster of important British artists signed to EMI in the
'70s and '80s, including Kate Bush, The Sex Pistols (who lasted
for about three months, released one single and subsequently
wrote the track 'EMI' in honour of their brief deal), Olivia Newton-
John, Sheena Easton, Iron Maiden, The Rolling Stones and
Duran Duran. At the same time, EMI became home to a new
breed of TV-advertised compilation albums which ultimately
led to the *Now That's What I Call Music* series launched in
partnership with Virgin. The famous title for these compilation
albums – which have been produced for nearly 20 years – is
said to have come from a Danish ministry of agriculture poster
in Virgin's offices, which showed a pig listening to a cockerel
crowing and thinking: 'Now that's what I call music.'

No 1
Singles **8**
Albums **2**

No 1
Singles **31**
Albums **27**

EMI

During the 1990s, the EMI label was home to Eternal, Louise, Chumbawamba, Roxette and the former Spice Girl Geri Halliwell, while former Harvest stalwarts Pink Floyd also switched imprints. At the same time, the EMI Classics label – which was formed to replace HMV as its international classical brand in the '90s – now boasts many major names, such as Sir Simon Rattle, Nigel Kennedy, Itzhak Perlman and Dame Kiri Te Kanawa. The EMI label was resurrected in America, and between 1989 and 1991 it delivered a total of seven Number One hit singles from EMF, Richard Marx and Swedish band Roxette.

Also in the '90s, EMI and Chrysalis merged into a single pop division, which managed the labels Cooltempo, Harvest, Ensign, Positiva and the new in-house dance label Prolifica, while Heavenly Records also became part of the restructured EMI Records.

No 1
Singles **9**
Albums **2**

No 1
Singles **2**
Albums **2**

EMI-AMERICA

THE EMI COMPANY CREATED AND LAUNCHED EMI-AMERICA IN 1978 AS A SECOND US-BASED COMPANY THERE, alongside the established Capitol Records. Initial success came in the shape of Kim Carnes, Scotland's Sheena Easton (whose UK hit 'Nine To Five' became a US Number One under the title 'Morning Train' so that it wouldn't clash with Dolly Parton's hit of the same name), J Geils Band and $10 million signing David Bowie, who with Mick Jagger delivered 'Dancing In The Street' in support of Live Aid. The label also handled the Liberty imprint and roster following EMI's purchase of United Artists in 1979.

British-born singer John Waite delivered the last number on the LA-based EMI America label in 1984 with 'Missing You', and the label was closed down in the late '80s in order to make way for a new EMI label based in New York called Manhattan, which delivered Richard Marx and Bobby McFerrin before also being closed in the '90s.

EMI MUSIC

THE ONLY BRITISH COMPANY LISTED AMONG THE WORLD'S BIG FIVE MAJOR RECORD COMPANIES, EMI (Electric And Musical Industries) traces its origins back the Gramophone Company, which was founded in London in 1897 by the American William Barry Owen and his British partner, Trevor Williams.

The company's first offices were situated in Maiden Lane, in London's Covent Garden, where the first British studio recordings were made by producer Fred Gaisberg in 1898, including a version of 'Comin' Thru The Rye' sung by Syria Lamonte, a barmaid from the nearby Rules restaurant. American-born Gaisberg was the man who signed the world's first million-selling star – Italian tenor Enrico Caruso – to The Gramophone Company, paying the £100 advance from his own money after the company turned down his request for funds.

Registered as the Gramophone And Typewriter Company between 1900 and 1907, The Gramophone Company and its rival, Columbia Graphophone Company – whose combined sales of 30 million records in 1930 accounted for half of the total British record market – merged in 1931 to create EMI. The new company brought the HMV and Columbia labels together with European labels Parlophone, Electrola and Pathé, The China Record Company and India's GramCo to form an international business that ranked as the world's biggest record company for nearly 50 years.

EMI opened the famous Abbey Road studios in 1931, while in-house scientist Alan Dower Blumlein took out the first patents for stereo recording in 1933 and the company forged links with US labels RCA and CBS to release their recordings in the UK. EMI established and ran HMV record shops within its music division, alongside its major electrical, medical, film and leisure activities.

Sir Joseph Lockwood, who took over as Chairman of EMI in the '50s, was instrumental in maintaining EMI's position as Britain's most successful music company. He once remarked that, on joining the company, his first job was to go to bankers in the City of London and raise the £1 million necessary to pay the company's wage bill. He also ended the HMV franchise system, whereby only certain approved shops could sell HMV product, which allowed records from rival companies to be sold in the company's flagship HMV store in Oxford Street.

The American company Capitol Records was acquired in 1955, at a time when the company's UK arm was losing its rights to successful American repertoire from CBS and RCA, among others. EMI responded by becoming the leading light during the '60s, Britain's golden decade of pop music.

On the heels of an unsuccessful bid for EMI Music by the Paramount division of US giants Gulf And Western, the company acquired the United Artists record company in 1979, just before being taken over by UK electrical giant Thorn. EMI Music then bought Chrysalis Records in 1991, and paid Richard Branson over £500 million for his Virgin Music Group in 1992. The parent Thorn EMI Company de-merged in 1996 to create The EMI Group and the Thorn Company.

Today, EMI Music has dropped down in the world rankings, operating the EMI, Parlophone, Harvest, Chrysalis, Capitol, Angel, EMI Classics, HMV, Blue Note, Liberty, United Artists, Virgin, Innocent and Hut labels, alongside EMI Music Publishing. A planned merger with Warner Music Group – announced in early 2000 – was abandoned the same year and the company set about combining its own EMI and Virgin operations around the world.

US No 1
Singles **1**
Albums **1**

UK No 1
Singles **3**
Albums **1**

ENSIGN

FORMER PHONOGRAM A&R EXECUTIVE NIGEL GRAINGE CREATED ENSIGN IN 1976 when he was offered the chance to start his own label as an incentive to stay with the company. He took the offer, and settled originally on the name N Sign (as in Nigel's Sign).

Joined by former Phonogram colleague and DJ Chris Hill, Grainge delivered Ensign's first hits in 1977 with The Boomtown Rats, whose frontman was Bob Geldof, the man who went on to mastermind Band Aid and Live Aid. The label's interest in the growing UK black music scene resulted in hits for Black Slate, Light Of The World and Eddy Grant before Grainge sold The Boomtown Rats to Phonogram in 1983 and was given the Ensign label in exchange.

Working through Island Records, Ensign emerged once again with the artists Phil Fearon and Flash And The Pan, but in 1984 Grainge decided to sell his label. However, even after Chrysalis had bought Ensign, Grainge continued to run the label and bolstered its value by signing The Waterboys, World Party and Sinéad O'Connor.

When EMI acquired half of Chrysalis in 1989, this included the Ensign label, which was still being run by Grainge. However, following EMI's purchase of the remaining 50% in 1991, Ensign's founder took his leave of the company that he created. 'Things had begun to go wrong in the last years leading up to EMI's final buy-out, and then there was a new corporate attitude which I didn't really get on with,' he says, recalling his departure. Ensign remains within the EMI Chrysalis division but is a largely unused identity.

No 1
Singles **45**
Albums **22**

No 1
Singles **51**
Albums **33**

EPIC

THE LABEL THAT IS HOME TO THE WORLD'S BEST SELLING ALBUM OF ALL TIME – Michael Jackson's *Thriller* – was launched by CBS in 1953 as a jazz and classical label offering the likes of The Juilliard String Quartet and The Berlin Philharmonic Orchestra. Epic's first major success came from Bobby Vinton, who racked up four US Number One singles and established the label's name. Next came a wave of '60s British acts, when Epic acquired The Dave Clark Five, The Hollies, Donovan, The Yardbirds, Lulu and Jeff Beck in America.

Operating alongside the more established CBS label, Epic branched out in the late '60s and early '70s into soul, reggae, rock and country with artists such as Sly And The Family Stone, Johnny Nash, The Isley Brothers, Edgar Winter and Charlie Rich. In 1976, Epic also signed a famous quintet from Motown Records. The Jackson 5 soon became The Jacksons, and two years later Michael Jackson launched his historic solo career on the label, including the release of the album *Thriller*, the world's best-selling album at over 50 million copies.

A wide range of artists – from Ozzy Osbourne, Sade and REO Speedwagon to Luther Vandross, Gloria Estefan and Cyndi Lauper, who later appeared on the sister label Portrait – succeeded in maintaining Epic's high profile. After British duo Wham! had delivered their hits, a solo George Michael carried the Epic banner until his highly-publicised split with the parent Sony corporation in 1995.

Epic soldiered on, however, and held onto its important position within Sony, who had purchased the CBS Records division – including Epic – in 1988, adding a wide range of contemporary acts including Rage Against the Machine, Macy Gray, multi-million selling Canadian superstar Celine Dion (on the 550/Epic imprint), Latin star Jennifer Lopez, Mudvayne and Big Brovaz.

Epitaph

EPITAPH

BRETT GUREWITZ, GUITARIST WITH PUNK BAND BAD RELIGION, SET UP EPITAPH RECORDS IN 1981 as an outlet for his own band's releases. New acts soon followed including Offspring – whose 4 million-selling début album was the label's first mainstream success – Rancid, Dropkick Mule and UK star Tricky.

Epitaph continued to expand, adding the Anti- imprint, featuring Merle Haggard and Tom Waits, and the distribution of blues label Fat Possum, and is now listed as one of the world's top 30 independent record companies.

ERATO

THE ORIGINAL FRENCH CLASSICAL LABEL ERATO
DATES BACK TO 1881, although the more familiar Erato
Disques was founded in 1953 to promote French baroque
music while also launching the careers of leading French artists
such as Marie-Claire Alain.

In 1992, when it became part of the Warner Classics
International operation, Erato boasted William Christie, Daniel
Barenboim and Ton Koopman on its roster. Since then it has
grown to include leading tenors Jose Carreras and Jose Cura
alongside singers Dawn Upshaw, Misia, Sumi Jo and Filippa
Giordano, and Erato launched the subsidiary label Detour to
manage their world music releases in 1999.

ECHO – see Chrysalis Group

END – see Roulette

ENJOY – see Fury/Fire/Enjoy

ESSENTIAL – see London

ETERNAL – see WEA

EXCEL – see Philadelphia International

No 1
Singles -
Albums -

No 1
Singles **1**
Albums **1**

Factory

F

FACTORY

FOLLOWING A DISTINCTLY UNIQUE ROUTE WHICH DIDN'T INCLUDE SUCH TRADITIONAL RECORD COMPANY TRAPPINGS AS CONTRACTS AND ADVANCES, Factory Records emerged out of Manchester's renewed and sometimes hectic music business in 1978. Cambridge graduate turned TV presenter and producer Tony Wilson was the leading light behind Factory Records and the short-lived Factory Club. The Durutti Column – who were managed by Wilson and partner Alan Erasmus – launched the label, but the first taste of success came with Joy Division, OMD, James and New Order, which then led to the opening of the notorious Hacienda Club.

Despite a host of hit records, Factory suffered drastically when their un-contracted bands started to leave, and even though new acts broke through, such as The Happy Mondays, the label was in serious financial straits by the early '90s. While an attempt to sell the label fell through, both New Order and The Happy Mondays sold their catalogues before splitting up and Wilson was forced to dissolve the label in 1993, although the sequel, Factory Too, made a brief appearance in the mid '90s.

Fantasy

No 1
Singles -
Albums **2**

No 1
Singles -
Albums -

FANTASY

FANTASY RECORDS GREW FROM A PLASTIC MOULDING AND RECORD-PRESSING BUSINESS IN SAN FRANCISCO – with jazz pianist Dave Brubeck amongst its clients – into one of the most important reissue companies in the world. Formed by Max and Sol Weiss in 1949 and named after a sci-fi magazine, Fantasy went on to sign Brubeck, along with Gerry Mulligan and comedian Lenny Bruce. In 1968, Fantasy executive Saul Zaentz and a group of investors bought the label, relocated to Berkeley in California and successfully moved into rock music, releasing material by Creedence Clearwater Revival

Adding soul and disco artists to the label such as The Blackbyrds, Sylvester and Ruth Brown, Fantasy grew and began to acquire the catalogues of smaller American jazz labels such as Contemporary, Prestige, Riverside, Milestone, Good Time and Pablo. They also re-opened the subsidiary label Galaxy (also named after a sci-fi magazine) in 1978 to release new recordings by the likes of Tommy Flanagan and Art Pepper.

The closure of Galaxy in the mid '80s confirmed Fantasy's commitment to playing its role as a re-issues company, delivering titles first issued by Blue Note, Keynote and Dr Jazz, along with original Creedence albums and the Stax catalogue, which featured Willie Dixon and The Staples Singers. New jazz releases from the '90s have also appeared on the Fantasy label, including The Vince Guaraldi Trio.

FESTIVAL
MUSHROOM
RECORDS

FESTIVAL MUSHROOM

FESTIVAL RECORDS EMERGED OUT OF an Australian custom-pressing operation based in Sydney called Casper Precision Engineering.

Owner Paul Cullen saw the potential for an Australian record company and launched Festival Records in 1952. Early releases included band leader Leslie Welch and US rock 'n' roll star Bill Haley's 'Rock Around The Clock', while Johnny O'Keefe became the label's first local rock signing in 1957.

In 1961 Rupert Murdoch's News Corporation bought Festival Records, which at various times included on its artists' roster the likes of Olivia Newton-John, Peter Allen, Rolf Harris and The Bee Gees. Throughout the '70s and '80s, records from distinguished labels such as Atlantic, A&M, Chrysalis, Island, Stiff and Virgin were distributed 'down-under' by Festival and, more recently, the company represented labels including Fantasy, Gut, Rykodisc and Walt Disney.

Festival bought an interest in the successful local company Mushroom in 1993 and in 1998 took 100% control of the label, merging it with Festival which was by now under the control of James Murdoch, who also launched the Rawkus label in America.

After selling Both Rawkus and Mushroom Records UK, Festival Mushroom retains an extensive Australian catalogue, including established local artists such as Kylie Minogue, Jimmy Barnes and Paul Kelly plus new signings george, 28 Days and Motor Ace.

FLIP

JORDAN SCHUR MANAGED ACTS AND BOOKED LOCAL SHOWS WHILE AT COLLEGE IN BOSTON BEFORE STARTING HIS OWN CALIFORNIAN LABEL IN 1994. Flip Records has grown into a multi-million-dollar company specialising in rock bands like million-sellers Limp Bizkit, Stained and Dope. Setting up individual joint-venture deals with larger companies for each act, Flip continues under the control of founder Schur, despite his position as president of Geffen Records. By way of a tribute to Geffen band Nirvana, Schur explains: 'I started Flip the day Kurt Cobain died because I wanted to help fill the void left by his death.'

No 1
Singles -
Albums -

No 1
Singles **2**
Albums **3**

FLY

FLY WAS ESTABLISHED BY MUSIC PUBLISHER DAVID PLATZ IN THE LATE '60s and benefited from the decision made by producers Denny Cordell and Tony Visconti to switch their allegiance, moving their artists from EMI's Regal Zonophone label to the new and independent Fly label. Joe Cocker, The Move and Procol Harum were all involved in the decision to move, but the label's only major success followed Marc Bolan's decision to abbreviate the name of his group from Tyrannosaurus Rex to T Rex, after which the band went on to deliver Number One albums and singles before moving back to EMI in 1972. Meanwhile, The Move appeared on the Harvest imprint.

John Kongos also delivered hits for Fly, which was joined by the Cube label (home to Joan Armatrading's first recordings) in 1973. Fly and Cube recordings remain in the Platz family and have been regularly repackaged.

No 1
Singles **4**
Albums -

No 1
Singles **5**
Albums **3**

FONTANA

FONTANA BEGAN LIFE AS AN INDEPENDENT LABEL IN FRANCE BEFORE EMERGING IN THE '60s as part of the Philips company and featuring UK chart acts such as Manfred Mann, Dave Dee, Dozy, Beaky, Mick and Tich, The Spencer Davis Group and, most appropriately, the Manchester group singer named Wayne Fontana, who reportedly took his name not from the label but from Elvis Presley's drummer, DJ Fontana.

American Vanguard acts such as Joan Baez and Country Joe And The Fish appeared in the UK on Fontana while major UK acts The Who, Led Zeppelin and Slade all initially appeared on the label without success as The High Numbers, Jimmy Page and Ambrosia Slade respectively. The label missed the chance of a major European hit in 1969 when the controversial single 'Je T'Aime...Moi Non Plus' by Jane Birkin and Serge Gainsbourg was dropped from the label after being banned from British radio and television, who branded it obscene. It was later picked up by the independent Major Minor label.

When Philips revamped their UK music operations, Fontana disappeared and was replaced in the late '60s by the Vertigo and Mercury labels. However, subsequent artists Tears For Fears, Was (Not Was), Oleta Adams and James re-activated the Fontana label and re-affirmed its chart presence in the last decade as part of Universal's Mercury division.

No 1
Singles -
Albums -

No 1
Singles **2**
Albums **4**

FOOD

EX-MUSICIAN DAVID BALFE AND EX-MUSIC JOURNALIST ANDY ROSS SET UP FOOD RECORDS IN 1984. Balfe had previously cut his teeth by playing with The Teardrop Explodes and managing Strawberry Switchblade and Brilliant (which featured KLF's Jimmie Cauty), while Ross wrote for Sounds until its closure in 1992. The pair joined forces at Food in 1985 and then became co-managers of Ross' discovery Voice Of The Beehive before entering into a long-term affiliation with EMI Records in 1988, through which they obtained the necessary funding to allow the label to discover and develop new artists.

Food's initial success came in 1985 with Brilliant's first hit, but it was Jesus Jones who established the label when they became the first UK indie act to top a US chart. They were closely followed on the path of success by Blur, who took the Food label to new heights, winning a record four Brit awards in one year.

Balfe and Ross finally sold their shares in the label to EMI in 1994 when Balfe withdrew from the label, leaving Ross to run the EMI-owned company from the label's north London offices. Ross has commented that they complemented each other as partners: 'David was interested in selling shit-loads of records while I was interested in the integrity of indie music.'

Operating under the control of EMI, Food went on to sign Shampoo, who in Japan were million-selling artists, and the label continues to search for new British talent to add to the Food menu alongside best-sellers Blur.

No 1
Singles -
Albums -

No 1
Singles 1
Albums -

4AD

BEGGARS BANQUET STAFFERS IVO WATTS-RUSSELL AND PETER KENT LAUNCHED AXIS RECORDS IN 1980, and among their first artists were original signings Bauhaus. A name change to 4AD along with a loan from Beggars Banquet ensured the label's progress, led to the signing of Modern English, The The and The Birthday Party, and forged an on-going link with the Banquet organisation. The capture and success of The Cocteau Twins established 4AD as both a credible and commercial label and brought The Pixies and American UK chart-toppers M/A/R/R/S into the stable.

Despite Top Ten albums from Lush and Belly in the first half of the '90s, 4AD couldn't maintain its previous level of commercial success, although the label remains a credible home for new acts such as Gus Gus and Mojave 3, who remain under the Beggars Banquet umbrella.

No 1
Singles **1**
Albums -

No 1
Singles -
Albums -

FURY/FIRE/ENJOY

BOBBY ROBINSON, THE FOUNDER OF THE FURY, FIRE AND ENJOY RECORD LABELS, served his apprenticeship as the owner of a record shop in the Harlem district of New York in the '40s before working as a talent scout, producer and label owner throughout the '50s.

The first Robinson labels, some of which involved brother Danny, were Red Robin and Whirlin' Disc, before Fury was set up in 1957. Among early signings were a young Gladys Knight And The Pips, who brought the label R&B chart success before they moved on to Motown. Wilbert Harrison's version of 'Kansas City', produced by Robinson, earned Fury its only US Number One hit, but as Harrison was already under contract to a rival label Fury became the subject of prolonged litigation.

More than 15 years after starting the label, Robinson began to focus on the early rap movement of the late '70s, launching Grandmaster Flash and Funky Four Plus One before going on to record Doug E Fresh and Dr Ice.

Following Flash's move to Sylvia Robinson's (no relation) Sugarhill, Robinson returned to retailing and ran down both his recording interests and his record labels.

FALCON – see Vee Jay

F BEAT – see Demon

FEDERAL – see King

FEINERY – see Concord

FFRR – see London

FIRE – see Fury/Fire/Enjoy

FIRST AVENUE – see Arista

550 – see Epic

FONOVISA – see Universal

FOURTH AND BROADWAY – see Island

FSUK – see Ministry Of Sound

G

GALLO

SOUTH AFRICAN ENTREPRENEUR ERIC GALLO BEGAN HIS MUSIC PUBLISHING, RETAILING AND IMPORTING BUSINESS IN 1926 with the formation of Brunswick Gramophone House. By the late 1980s, the Gallo Africa company reportedly operation-owned over 80% of all recordings made in South Africa.

Having originally distributed American Brunswick releases in South Africa, Gallo set up the Singer Gramophone company in 1930 to record local talent, and also distributed Decca Records releases from the likes of Bing Crosby, Ella Fitzgerald and Louis Jordan.

In 1946, Gallo combined all his operations under the name Gallo Africa, which was then listed on the Johannesburg stock exchange. The company set about recording emerging black and white artists in South Africa for their new Gallotone label, the Mavuthela Music imprint and Gramophone and Trutone labels. The Singer imprint was phased out under threat of legal action by the Singer Sewing Machine Company.

In 1976, Gallo Africa acquired 50% of local Teal Records and merged the two operations. When Eric Gallo retired in 1980, he sold Gallo to Anglo America's Premier Milling Company which merged Gallo Africa with the CNA retail chain in 1982. The local RPM Records was added in 1981, Teal Trutone Records was formed (within a 50/50 partnership with Polygram) and, in 1988, the Gramophone and Gallo operations were consolidated into Gallo GRC, which promoted local music and also acted as a licensee for many of the world's leading labels.

In 1997, local Tusk Music was added to a Gallo Group which, post-apartheid, was much reduced and was part of Johnnic Entertainment, but still boasted leading local artists such as Ladysmith Black Mambazo, Soul Brothers And Lusanda Spiritual Group and Joe Nina.

GEFFEN

No 1
Singles **5**
Albums **12**

No 1
Singles **4**
Albums **5**

GEFFEN

AFTER A FOUR-YEAR ABSENCE FROM THE MUSIC BUSINESS DUE TO ILL HEALTH, David Geffen returned to start his eponymous label in 1980, the second record company that he had launched in the space of a decade.

US music industry legend Geffen had founded Asylum in 1970 and had controlled the combined Elektra/Asylum company before his enforced sabbatical in the mid '70s. He founded his second label with financial assistance from the Warner Communications corporation (owners of Elektra/Asylum), and later commented: 'When I started Asylum they said you couldn't start a record company from scratch. Then, when I started Geffen, they said I wouldn't be able to do it again. But Geffen Records is probably as profitable a record company as any in the world.'

Elton John and Donna Summer were among the first superstar signings to the LA-based company, but the world's attention became focused on the label after the release of John Lennon's last studio album, *Double Fantasy*, in 1980. Geffen added major acts for a further decade with varying degrees of success, including Cher, Kylie Minogue, Don Henley, Guns N' Roses and Aerosmith, before Geffen sold his label to MCA for stock worth a reported $550 million. By the time it was sold to MCA, Geffen's empire also included Geffen Films (which made *Little Shop Of Horrors*) and a Broadway production company, which produced *Cats* and *Dreamgirls*. Under MCA's ownership, David Geffen remained chairman of the record company and introduced the subsidiary label DGC, which hit the sales jackpot with Hole, Beck and Seattle grunge band Nirvana.

Geffen left the company that he named after himself in 1995, and Geffen Records eventually became part of the huge Universal Music Group. Following cuts in staff and the artists' roster, the label is now part of the Interscope/Geffen/A&M division, where it boasts acts such as Counting Crows, Lisa Loeb, Cold and multi-million sellers Limp Bizkit.

No 1
Singles **2**
Albums -

No 1
Singles **1**
Albums -

GIANT

IRVING AZOFF, MANAGER OF THE EAGLES AND JACKSON BROWNE, was named head of MCA in 1983, and three years later he sold his own management, record label and merchandising companies to MCA for a reported $15.7 million. After leaving MCA he formed his own Giant label in LA in 1990, and the music industry speculated that Azoff chose the name Giant as a joke because of his diminutive stature.

Color Me Badd established the label's presence in 1991 with the US Number One single 'I Adore Mi Amor' and the UK chart-topper 'I Want To Sex You Up'. When Azoff opened up the subsidiary label Revolution in 1996, Giant shifted their attention to focus on country music, with Clay Walker And The Wilkinsons making an impression.

Financed as a joint venture with Warner Bros Records, Giant added a re-formed Steely Dan to their roster before becoming part of Reprise Records.

No 1
Singles -
Albums -

No 1
Singles **5**
Albums **5**

GO! DISCS

FOUNDED IN 1983 BY ANDY MACDONALD, with an initial loan investment of £1,500, Go! Discs first saw chart action in 1985 with Billy Bragg and his EP *Between The Wars*. Within a year, The Housemartins added considerably to the label's status with their hits 'Happy Hour' and 'Caravan Of Love' (the label's first Number One record), attracting the interest of Polygram, who bought a minority stake in the label in 1987.

After The Housemartins split and evolved into The Beautiful South in 1989, they became the label's first million-selling artists, while Beats International emerged under the direction of former Housemartin Norman Cook, later to become Fatboy Slim. The sister dance label Go! Beat was set up at the start of the '90s and delivered major sellers Gabrielle and Portishead.

A minor setback in Go! Discs' fortunes was offset with the emergence of ex-Jam frontman Paul Weller on the label in 1992 and his consequent string of best-selling hit releases. Along with album chart-toppers The Beautiful South, he helped to re-establish the label's prominent position in the mid '90s. However, McDonald fell out with partners Polygram and resigned from the company in 1996, when the major acquired the outstanding 51% from the label's founder. McDonald claimed that his departure had been forced on him by Polygram, who continue to operate the Go! Beat label.

GRAND ROYAL

GROUND-BREAKING WHITE RAP GROUP THE BEASTIE BOYS LAUNCHED THEIR OWN LABEL IN 1992 as a platform for the release of their third album. Adam Horovitz, Adam Yauch and Mike Diamond emerged out of New York City in 1986 with the record-breaking, multi-million-selling début album *Licensed To Ill*. Originally signed to Def Jam records, The Beastie Boys left acrimoniously, suing the label for alleged unpaid royalties, and after they linked with Capitol Records they proceeded to set up the Grand Royal label.

In addition to releasing The Beastie Boys' albums, Grand Royal has also become home to Sean Ono Lennon, son of John and Yoko.

Great Records
Period

GRP

MUSICIANS AND PIONEERING RECORDING
TECHNICIANS Dave Grusin and Larry Rosen set up GRP
Records in New York in 1982 as an 'all-digital' MOR and jazz
label. Working both alone and as partners, the pair had been
involved with Andy Williams, Patti Austin and Earl Klugh before
they caught the digital/compact disc bug and proceeded to
record George Benson, Lee Ritenour, Michael Brecker,
Spirogyra, Special EFX and Grusin himself on their GRP and
Impulse labels.

Catalogue product from jazz greats such as Billie Holiday,
Count Basie, John Coltrane and Dizzy Gillespie added value
to GRP, and in 1990 the label was acquired by the Universal
Music Group. Since then, new jazz releases featuring Joe
Sample and George Benson have re-established the GRP name
among the list of leading jazz labels.

No 1
Singles -
Albums -

No 1
Singles **1**
Albums **2**

GUT

LAUNCHED IN 1988 AS THE GUT REACTION PROMOTION COMPANY, the company's biggest success came in 1991 with Right Said Fred, who appeared on the backwards-spelled subsidiary Tug label. Former EMI and Arista promotion man Guy Holmes hit the jackpot with the worldwide Number One single 'I'm Too Sexy' and the band's five-million-selling début album, *Right Said Fred*. Homes actually paid £1,000 for the mastering of 'I'm Too Sexy' with the intention of selling it to a major and splitting the profits with the band. When it was rejected, however, Holmes decided to set up Tug Records and released the record himself.

In 1996, Gut Records was formally named and launched by the band Space, who have since been joined by Jimmy Somerville, Sound 5, Avenging Angels and Naomi. In 1998, veteran singer Tom Jones signed to Gut and took the label back to the top with his Number One 1999 album *Reload*, which features duets with the likes of Robbie Williams, Catatonia's Cerys Matthews and The Cardigans. While Jones left the label, Gut forged a new UK partnership with US label Tommy Boy Records.

GALAXY – see Fantasy

GAMBLE – see Philadelphia International

GEE STREET – see V2

GLORY – see King

GLOWWORM – see Epic

GO! BEAT – see Go! Discs

GOLDEN GUINEA – see Pye

GONE – see Roulette

GORDY – see Motown

GRAMAVISION – see Rykodisc

GREGMARK – see Philles

GUSTO – see King

No 1
Singles -
Albums **1**

No 1
Singles **3**
Albums **5**

HARVEST

MANCHESTER UNIVERSITY GRADUATE CUM EMI TRAINEE MANAGER MALCOLM JONES was the brains behind the creation of the UK's leading progressive label back in 1969, when he persuaded his masters that EMI's existing labels were not appropriate outlets for the emerging underground music. While former Beatles engineer and Parlophone label manager Norman Smith was nominally in charge of Harvest, it was Jones who saw that EMI needed a new label in order to compete with the likes of Vertigo and Deram (launched by Philips and Decca respectively).

Harvest was launched by The Edgar Broughton Band in 1969, who were closely followed by Deep Purple, but it was a group whose first two hit singles and three albums appeared on EMI's Columbia label who were to make the label a household name. Pink Floyd's first Harvest album was produced by Smith, and their 1973 release *Dark Side Of The Moon* went on to become the best selling album by a British group, with total sales in excess of 25 million. Artists such as Kevin Ayers, Roy Harper and Barclay James Harvest all emerged from Harvest, as did The Electric Light Orchestra and Wizzard.

Revolutionary album sleeve designs and marketing campaigns were also part of the Harvest image, which was maintained by the likes of Soft Machine and Be Bop Deluxe, alongside late-'70s punk bands Wire and Saints and Top Three singles act Marshall Hain. Appropriately enough, Harvest's last Number One single came with Pink Floyd's 'Another Brick In The Wall (Part 2)' in 1979, and the group's 1983 release *The Final Cut* was the last chart-topping album released by the label. When Floyd moved over to the EMI label, Harvest became little more than a vehicle for re-issues, and today remains an under-used part of EMI.

Heavenly

US
No 1
Singles -
Albums -

UK
No 1
Singles -
Albums 1

HEAVENLY

LAUNCHED IN 1990 BY JEFF BARRETT, Heavenly Records became home to such notable British artists as Saint Etienne, Doves, the Manic Street Preachers and Beth Orton.

New artists such as The Vines, Ed Harcourt and Starsailor have maintained Heavenly's standing as a major talent source while the label strengthened its ties with EMI.

Barrett retained close ties with his label, including artist management links, while launching a trio of clubs/bars called The Social.

No 1
Singles **1**
Albums -

No 1
Singles -
Albums -

RECORDS

HI

HI (HIT INSTRUMENTALS) RECORDS SPRANG UP IN MEMPHIS IN 1957 as the brainchild of local rockabilly star Ray Harris. After early hits from the Bill Black Combo (led by Elvis Presley's original bass player, who quit to form his own group because of low pay), and then from sax player Ace Cannon, Hi Records emerged in the '60s as a soul label based around house bandleader and singer Willie Mitchell.

In 1970, Mitchell bought Hi Records and brought soul/gospel legend Al Green to the label. The combination of Green's voice and Mitchell's high-quality arrangments and production earned Hi seven US Top Ten singles by Green. Ann Peebles was a later addition to the roster before Hi was sold to Cream Records, but the label failed to find success. Today the catalogue is represented by the Demon label in the UK.

HMV

HMV'S DOG-AND-TRUMPET LOGO IS PROBABLY THE MOST FAMOUS TRADEMARK IN THE INTERNATIONAL MUSIC BUSINESS, and its design began with a painting of a fox terrier listening to a phonograph. Artist Francis Barraud produced the original painting in 1889, using his brother's dog, Nipper, and an early cylinder machine, titling it 'His Master's Voice'. The Gramophone Company later agreed to purchase the copyright for £50, and the painting for a further £50, subject to Barraud repainting it with a new model gramophone replacing the phonograph.

In 1890, the dog-and-trumpet logo began to appear on the Gramophone Company's records in the UK released on the Black label, while Emile Berliner (the inventor of the gramophone) secured the rights to the His Master's Voice trademark in America and Canada. When ER Johnson took over his business, the HMV trademark was used for his new Victor Talking Machine Company, which in 1904 obtained the rights to HMV in Japan.

While the Gramophone Company registered both the words 'His Master's Voice' and the picture in the UK in 1910, it had experienced difficulties in introducing the logo around the world. In Russia, Egypt, India and Moslem countries, the dog was considered to be an unclean animal, and alternatives such as a cobra were used in India. Italy, too, was a problem for Nipper, as in that country a bad singer was said to sing like a dog.

In 1922, when the Gramophone Company used the HMV logo to herald the opening of their British Sales And Zonophones store and head office in London's Oxford Street, it quickly became known as the HMV shop.

By the time of the merger with Columbia in 1931 that led to the formation of EMI, HMV was already established as the premier international classical label within the Gramophone Company. It continued to focus on releasing classical recordings until the '50s, along with records by stars from British music hall, radio and films.

EMI's distribution of records from the American RCA company (owners of HMV in the US) resulted in the fact that stars such as Eddie Fisher – and, most noticeably, Elvis Presley – actually appeared on HMV in the UK. The expiration of these deals

HMV

required HMV to establish its own roster of new British talent, and the success of Alma Cogan, Johnny Kidd And The Pirates and Danny Williams paved the way for '60s groups The Swinging Blue Jeans and Manfred Mann.

In the '70s, with EMI's pop records being released on Parlophone, EMI and Harvest, HMV reverted to its status as a classical label, enjoying chart success with Sarah Brightman's 'Pie Jesu', from Andrew Lloyd Webber's 1985 *Requiem*. Former Smiths man Morrissey had the label re-activated as part of his EMI contract, and between 1988 and 1992 he charted with 14 HMV singles before HMV was downgraded because of the lack of international rights. Because of the need for the central manufacturing of compact discs, EMI replaced HMV with the EMI Classics label, which they could use worldwide.

Today, the HMV name remains in constant use as the brand name of the EMI Group's worldwide chain of record stores. These stores use only the name HMV in America, Canada and Japan, under agreement with General Electric and JVC, but both the HMV name plus the dog-and-trumpet logo around the rest of the world.

Hollywood
RECORDS

No 1
Singles -
Albums **3**

No 1
Singles -
Albums -

HOLLYWOOD

THE RECORDING OFFSHOOT OF THE LEGENDARY WALT DISNEY CORPORATION, Hollywood Records celebrated its tenth anniversary in 1999. The label failed to make a major impact with early signings such as Party, The Brian Setzer Orchestra (formed by the ex-Stray Cats frontman) and Danzig, but it managed to acquire the US rights to British rock giants Queen, who provided the label with its only platinum or gold albums during its first nine years of business.

A major revamping of the label in 1998, when nearly a dozen acts were dropped, opened up the way for Fastball and Jennifer Paige to earn major sales for Hollywood, which operates alongside sister labels Lyric Street, Mammoth and soundtrack outlet Walt Disney Records as part of the Disney Corporation's Buena Vista Music Group.

No 1
Singles -
Albums -

No 1
Singles **1**
Albums **3**

HUT

ESTABLISHED IN 1990 as a wholly-owned subsidiary of Virgin, Hut began life in a small flat in London's trendy Portobello Road with a couple of unsuccessful Virgin acts.

Hut chief David Boyd, a former employee at Rough Trade distribution, inherited the acts Moose and Revolver when he launched the label two years before EMI acquired Virgin. Inspired by Elektra Records in America and the original Virgin label, he intended to establish Hut as a boutique label, boasting a select roster of acts. Taking its name from the hut at the main Virgin offices in which security and transportation operations were based ('It was part of the company but not part of the main building,' explains Boyd), Hut expanded their dealings with a selection of new acts, including The Smashing Pumpkins, who were licensed to Hut from the American Caroline label.

New British acts were soon signed, including Placebo, Embrace, David McAlmont, Gomez and The Verve, whose 7.5 million-selling album Urban Hymns stands as Hut's best-selling release to date. When the band split, leader Richard Ashcroft continued with the label.

hyperion

HYPERION

THE BRAINS BEHIND HYPERION, the UK's leading alternative classical record label, is a former south London minicab driver who learnt about classical music by working in specialist record shops. Edward Perry set up Hyperion (named after the father of the Muses in Greek mythology) in 1980 in order to record early Hildegard work from the twelfth century. Boasting more prestigious Gramophone awards than any other independent label, Hyperion has gone on to issue highly-praised recordings of performances of Handel, Liszt, Schubert and over 50 volumes of the complete piano music of Franz Liszt. In 2003, Hyperion's founder and Managing Director Perry died aged 71.

H&L – see Avco

HANNIBAL – see Rykodisc

HIGH STREET – see Windham Hill

HIGHER GROUND – see Sony Music

HIP-O – see Universal

HIT – see Chrysalis Group

HOT WAX – see Invictus

IMMEDIATE

US No 1
Singles -
Albums -

UK No 1
Singles 2
Albums 1

IMMEDIATE

ANDREW LOOG OLDHAM FAILED AS A POP STAR but succeeded in becoming manager of The Rolling Stones prior to the release of their first record in 1963. He went on to form his own Immediate label in 1965, with the help of publicist Tony Calder.

The label's first chart entry came with the UK release of the American hit 'Hang On Sloopy' by The McCoys. The acts signed to Immediate during the next three years included The Small Faces (who were also managed by Oldham), The Poets, the pre-Velvet Underground Nico, Chris Farlowe, The Nice and Amen Corner. Future Led Zeppelin star Jimmy Page also joined the label, as in-house producer.

The Small Faces' only Number One album, *Ogdens' Nut Gone Flake*, became a collector's item when it appeared on Immediate in 1968 with a round sleeve designed to resemble a tobacco tin. The idea came from one of the tobacco company's old tin designs for Ogden's Nut Brown Flake.

Having split from The Rolling Stones in 1967, Oldham then concentrated on Immediate. However, after limited success with groups Fleetwood Mac and Humble Pie, the label hit financial difficulties and was wound up in 1970. While the Immediate catalogue is still available today through Sanctuary Records, Oldham added to his own fortunes by collecting royalties from The Verve's 'Bitter Sweet Symphony' because it sampled The Rolling Stones' 'The Last Time', which he co-wrote.

No 1
Singles **3**
Albums **1**

No 1
Singles -
Albums -

IMPERIAL

IMPERIAL HAS BEEN A POPULAR NAME FOR RECORD LABELS SINCE THE EARLY YEARS OF THE 20TH CENTURY, when it first appeared as such in America. Other Imperial labels sprang up in the UK in the '20s, and also in Brazil and Holland, before Lew Chudd established the most famous Imperial label in Los Angeles in 1947.

Regarded as an influential label in the genre of R&B, Imperial's biggest hit came in 1952 with C&W star Slim Whitman, after which house producer Dave Bartholomew recruited Fats Domino to the label. With Domino at the head of the roster, Imperial went on to add Roy Brown and Smiley Lewis before moving into pop in 1957 with the discovery of Ricky Nelson, whose 'Poor Little Fool' earned Imperial the honour of having the Number One record in *Billboard*'s first Hot 100 singles chart in America in August 1958. In Britain, Domino, Nelson and drummer Sandy Nelson (no relation) appeared in the charts on the London label, which licensed Imperial for the UK.

After acquiring the Minit label in 1960, Chudd sold his company to Liberty in 1963. They maintained the label for UK acts in America, including Billy J Kramer, The Hollies and Georgie Fame, and also recruited Cher and Johnny Rivers to the roster. Following the takeover of Liberty/Imperial by United Artists in 1969, Imperial was phased out, although the label is still used to put out original re-issues through UA's owners, EMI Music.

independiente

No 1
Singles -
Albums -

No 1
Singles -
Albums **3**

INDEPENDIENTE

AFTER POLYGRAM ACQUIRED HIS ORIGINAL GO!
DISCS LABEL FOR A REPORTED £20 MILLION IN
1996, Andy Macdonald started all over again and set up a
new company, Independiente, in 1997. The small alternative
roster features Sun House, Firstborn, Deejay Punk, Roddy
Frame and million-selling, award-winning Scottish band Travis,
who brought the label its first major success with their album
The Man Who. Group frontman Fran Healy once recounted
how they came to join Independiente. 'I met with Andy
Macdonald when he didn't have a record label but he really
wanted to sign us, so he wrote out a personal cheque and
guaranteed to have a label for us to be on within in a year.'
Linked through Sony for distribution in the UK, Independiente's
releases are handled by the Epic operation in America. Paul
Weller split from the roster in 2003 after his album earned
the label its third UK Number One.

No 1
Singles **17**
Albums **13**

No 1
Singles **10**
Albums **4**

INTERSCOPE

JIMMY IOVINE WORKED AS ONE OF THE INDUSTRY'S LEADING RECORD ENGINEERS AND PRODUCERS, working with the likes of John Lennon, Bruce Springsteen, Patti Smith, Dire Straits, U2, Simple Minds and The Eurythmics before entering the business of running his own record label. He started the New-York-based Interscope label in 1990 with partner Ted Fields, receiving financial support from the Warner Music Group's Atlantic label, who owned 50% of the company. Early success came with signings Marky Mark and Primus, and in 1992 Iovine expanded the company's interests and provided financial support and distribution for the new Death Row label formed by Marion Knight which boasted a controversial rap roster including Snoop Doggy Dogg and 2Pac Shakur.

In 1995, under pressure from the American anti-rap movement, Warner Music was forced to end its association with Interscope and Death Row, with Fields and Iovine, buying back Warner Music's 50% share in the label. As they moved out of Warner, Fields exclaimed: 'We at Interscope will continue our tradition of providing a home for young and exciting artists.'

Within months, Interscope linked with the Universal Music Group, which acquired a 50% stake in the company. The new Interscope then added Ron Sexsmith, Bush, No Doubt and Blackstreet to its roster, while further links with TVT Records and Aftermath Entertainment brought Nine Inch Nails, Dr Dre and Eminem into the camp. Interscope finally severed its links with Death Row when the rap label formed a new association with Priority.

After Universal's purchase of Polygram Music, the label was merged with the Geffen and A&M labels and, under Iovine's continuing stewardship, brought forth chart toppers as diverse as Enrique Iglesias, Marilyn Manson, 50 Cents and Eminem, the world's top-selling artist in 2002.

Invictus Records

US	UK
No 1	No 1
Singles **1**	Singles **1**
Albums -	Albums -

INVICTUS

THE AMERICAN SOUL LABEL INVICTUS WAS CREATED IN 1968 by the leading composing and production team of Holland, Dozier and Holland, and in five short years the label delivered a string of hits from acts including The Chairmen Of The Board, along with Number One records from Freda Payne And The Honey Cones.

Brothers Eddie and Brian Holland and Lamont Dozier were at the forefront of the Motown sound in the '60s, creating hits for Marvin Gaye, Martha And The Vandellas, The Supremes, The Four Tops and The Isley Brothers. In 1967, seeking greater control and better rewards, they split from Motown and launched Invictus and its sister label, Hot Wax.

For contractual reasons, the label's first big hits in 1970 from Freda Payne and The Chairman Of The Board were credited to Dunbar and Wayne, but later releases carried the familiar Holland/Dozier/Holland nameplate. The two labels were wound down and closed in 1973 following Dozier's decision to leave and forge a solo career.

No 1
Singles **2**
Albums **2**

No 1
Singles **1**
Albums -

IRS

IRS'S FOUNDER, MILES COPELAND, combined a successful career as an artists' manager with the running of his own IRS record label, which was launched in the early '80s. The brother of Stewart, drummer with The Police, Miles looked after The Police, The Bangles and Sting.

All-girl group The Go-Go's – featuring Belinda Carlisle and Jane Wiedlin – were the label's first US chart-topping act, and they were followed by Doctor And The Medics in the UK. Georgia's most successful rock band, REM (who signed to IRS in 1982 and released their first six albums on IRS), was the label's most significant signing.

The label continued to succeed in America thanks to two 1989 Number Ones from UK band Fine Young Cannibals, and today the label is part of the global EMI Music empire.

ISLAND

ISLAND RECORDS, ONE OF THE WORLD'S MOST INFLUENTIAL INDEPENDENT RECORD COMPANIES, had two starts in life before settling down to deliver reggae maestro Bob Marley and Irish superstar group U2 onto the world stage.

Founder Chris Blackwell (whose family has links with the Crosse & Blackwell food empire) began his first Island company in Jamaica in 1959, taking the name from Alec Waugh's book *Island In The Sun*. Focusing on local jazz, R&B and reggae, Island's fortunes grew thanks to a successful business venture exporting records into the UK, which prompted Blackwell to move back to Britain and set up the first official Islands Records label in 1962.

In addition to distributing Jamaican music around London (mostly from the back of his Mini Cooper), Blackwell also set up a production company, which found success with teenage girl singer Millie's 'My Boy Lollipop' on Fontana in 1962, and also launched The Spencer Davis Group on the same label. At the same time, Island Records also established a range of small subsidiary labels – Surprise, Sue, Jump, Black Swan and Aladdin – to release comedy, R&B, soul, reggae, ska and pop records.

In an effort to break into the growing rock market, Blackwell first signed John Martyn and Traffic, and then added Fairport Convention, Cat Stevens, Jethro Tull, King Crimson, ELP and Free to the roster. He also joined forces with Lee Gopthal in 1968 to form the leading UK reggae label Trojan, although he sold his share four years later. However, he retained two important acts for Island: Bob Marley And The Wailers and Toots And The Maytals. In those early days, Blackwell judged a sale of around 30,000 copies of a first release to be a success, but later reflected that things had changed. 'No serious player in the business wants to waste their time with such a number. The music was once the reason for it all, but it's hardly in the equation any more. The numbers take over.'

Despite signing glam band Roxy Music and launching Island's new film business with The Harder They Come, the label suffered when production companies such as Chrysalis, Manticore and Bronze – who were responsible for some of the leading rock acts – set up their own labels. Returning to his roots, Blackwell decided to

No 1
Singles **5**
Albums **5**

No 1
Singles **7**
Albums **17**

ISLAND

concentrate on the work of Bob Marley. In 1975, he set off to America to launch Island US, which delivered hits from Joe South, War and Sparks.

Island Records entered the '80s with U2 at the helm of a roster which also featured Grace Jones, Robert Palmer and Stevie Winwood. They also boasted new subsidiary imprints Antilles, Mango and Fourth And Broadway, which focused on jazz, Afro/Jamaican and disco/dance music respectively. Major sales and controversy were brought to Island by way of a production deal with Liverpool group Frankie Goes To Hollywood, who were produced by former Island artist Trevor Horn and were signed to his ZTT label. (Horn, incidentally, was a Buggle in 1979.)

Island went on to be involved in the filming of *Kiss Of The Spider Woman* and *Mona Lisa*, and in 1987, 25 years after the start of Blackwell's UK business, Island's turnover topped $100 million. Two years later, Blackwell took the decision to sell his Island empire to Polygram for almost $300 million, while he remained at the helm of the label he had created to be 'the best – not the biggest – record company in the world.'

The '90s saw Island Records prosper under its new owners, with the likes of The Cranberries, PJ Harvey, Pulp and Dru Hill finding success, but Blackwell finally severed his links with Island and Polygram by resigning at the end of 1997. After the Universal Music Group acquired Polygram in 1999, Island's identity was further diminished when it was merged with the Def Jam and Mercury labels, but UK group The Sugababes brought chart-topping success to the label in 2003, alongside stalwarts U2 and emerging UK act Daniel Bedingfield.

IN THE PAST – see Koch

ISLAND BLUE – see Universal

No 1
Singles 1
Albums 2

No 1
Singles -
Albums -

records

J

FOLLOWING HIS DEPARTURE FROM ARISTA
RECORDS, the label he founded in 1975, Clive Davis formed
J Records in a private joint venture with BMG Entertainment
(owners of Arista Records) in 2002.

After furthering the careers of Arista artists such as Whitney
Houston, Kenny G and Santana, Davis filled J's roster with the
likes of Luther Vandross, Busta Rhymes, Alicia Keys, Annie
Lennox and Rod Stewart, plus a partnership with Wyclef Jean's
YClef Records.

In 2000 BMG acquired Davis's 50% stake in J Records,
which had notched up its début US Number One album with
Alicia Keys' 8+ million-selling first release, and combined the
label with its own RCA label in a newly formed RCA Music Group,
under the chairmanship of Davis.

Singles -
Albums -

No 1
Singles **1**
Albums **2**

JET

MOST FAMOUSLY ASSOCIATED WITH MULTI-MILLION
SELLERS THE ELECTRIC LIGHT ORCHESTRA, Jet
Records was founded in the late '70s by veteran promoter,
manager and agent Don Arden, who enjoyed the epithet 'the
godfather of rock'.

Having worked with Gene Vincent, The Rolling Stones and
The Animals, and having managed the Small Faces and Amen
Corner, Arden then looked after The Move and ELO on EMI's
Harvest label. He then went on to set up Jet within United
Artists Records, which was home to Black Sabbath, Ozzy
Osbourne, Lynsey de Paul and ELO, whose last releases in
1983 signalled the end of Jet's brief reign.

No 1
Singles **3**
Albums **12**

No 1
Singles **12**
Albums **3**

JIVE

FOUNDED IN 1981 BY CLIVE CALDER, the Jive company boasts two of the world's biggest-selling artists on its flagship Jive label. A division of Zomba, the highest-ranked independent company in the world, Jive Records has seen The Backstreet Boys and Britney Spears sell over 30 million albums in America between 1989 and 1999.

Jive grew throughout is first decade, issuing hits from Tight Fit, A Flock Of Seagulls, Billy Ocean and Samantha Fox, and entered the '90s with US acts DJ Jazzy Jeff And The Fresh Prince (including movie and music star Will Smith) and R Kelly on its roster. A new subsidiary label, Silvertone (named after the cheap electric guitars sold by mail order in America in the '60s), was then launched. This label's roster originally included The Stone Roses and The Men They Couldn't Hang before John Lee Hooker, Sonic Boom and Plumb were added. A second subsidiary, the Pepper imprint, was launched in 1998.

The huge success of The Backstreet Boys – which began in 1996 – vindicated Calder's commitment to commercial rap as a pop genre, but he has acknowledged that business is not just about hit records. 'This company is not dependent on somebody having a big album or anything like that. This is a very strong company financially.'

Zomba secured the success of its own distribution services by purchasing 75% of the Pinnacle Group, which, under the leadership of Steve Mason, was established at the outlet for a host of independent labels, including Nude, Tommy Boy and Echo. Further success arrived in the shape of Pepper artists Shanks And Bigfoot and the pop act Steps, thanks to Jive's links with pop entrepreneur Peter Waterman (an early associate in the late '70s through the PWL label's Eastern Bloc and Unity). This group's UK success was followed by that of American teen sensation Britney Spears, the youngest act to have simultaneous Number One singles and albums in the USA. At just 17 years of age, she was also the youngest artist to pass the million sales mark for a single in the UK. Without a Number One record on either side of the Atlantic in 2002, Jive became part of BMG following its acquisition of Zomba and hit the top spots again in 2003 with R Kelly and Justin Timberlake, from earlier chart toppers 'N Sync.

JADE – see Milan

JUANA – see TK

JUDGEMENT – see Ruffhouse

JUKE BOX – see Speciality

JUMP – see Island

JUNIOR BOYS OWN – see V2

No 1
Singles **2**
Albums -

No 1
Singles -
Albums -

K

KAMA SUTRA

KAMA SUTRA BEGAN LIFE IN NEW YORK IN 1965 AS PART OF A COMPANY CALLED KS PRODUCTIONS, managed by founders Artie Ripp, Phil Steinberg, Hy Mizrahi and later Art Kass. John Sebastian's group The Lovin' Spoonful were the first act signed to the label and proved to be its mainstay until the owners merged Kama Sutra into their new label Buddah Records because they were unhappy with their distribution deal.

Kama Sutra was retained as an imprint in the early '70s with Stories and Sha Na Na both enjoying chart hits before the label disappeared within Buddah, whose last owners went bankrupt in 1976.

US
No 1
Singles **4**
Albums **1**

UK
No 1
Singles -
Albums -

KAPP

THE DRIVING FORCE BEHIND KAPP RECORDS WHEN IT WAS SET UP IN 1955 WAS DAVE KAPP, brother of Jack Kapp, who founded American Decca in 1934. After having stayed at Decca for six years after his brother's death in 1949, Dave Kapp quickly struck gold with the first release on the Kapp label: the US Number One 'Autumn Leaves' by Roger Williams.

Kapp's preference for MOR material led to the founding of the subsidiary label Leader, home for new rock recordings including the risqué Brian Hyland hit 'Itsy Bitsy Teenie Weenie Yellow Polka Dot Bikini'. Meanwhile, safer hits came from Jane Morgan, Ruby And The Romantics and Louis Armstrong, who charted in America on Kapp and in the UK on London, which was part of Decca. Armstrong's 1964 US and UK Number One 'Hello Dolly' remains one of only two songs from a Broadway show to top the US singles chart in the rock era.

Kapp sold his label to MCA in 1967, and the last major-selling artist to chart under the Kapp imprint was Cher in 1971, before she switched to the MCA label.

KING

CINCINNATI BUSINESSMAN SYD NATHAN DABBLED IN A VARIETY OF BUSINESSES IN THE '30S BEFORE HE OPENED A RADIO STORE, which led to him to open a record shop and ultimately his own record label, King Records, in 1943. King moved into records as a result of the payment of a debt, which was settled in old juke box records. He sold these at cut-price rates in his radio store, and when the business took off his next move was to open a proper record shop. Then, when he began to meet local musicians who dropped in to buy records, he launched his own label.

King's new enterprise included a pressing plant along with music publishing and sleeve printing operations. Early signings on the King label were mainly hillbilly artists, such as The Carlisle Brothers and The Delmore Brothers, while early R&B/soul releases went out on the Queen subsidiary.

In the '50s, King Records featured major black acts such as Roy Brown, Jack Dupree, Otis Williams and the ultimate soul star James Brown, who was signed to the sister label Federal for just $200, alongside Johnny Guitar Watson. King also acquired the Deluxe and Bethlehem labels, and released a range of jazz and gospel records. Nathan and Brown had a highly successful but, at times, uneasy relationship throughout their time together at King. Nathan liked to involve himself in his artists' choice of material, something which wasn't always appreciated by his acts.

King also set up joint publishing operations with his artists, which he then administered on their behalf – for a good fee. It acted as an incentive for his artists, who would receive more money from a joint deal with King than they would from a deal with outside publishers.

KING

Throughout the '60s, Brown carried the King banner almost single-handedly, issuing million-selling singles and a total of nine chart albums between 1964 and 1969. Following Nathan's death in 1968, the label was sold to Hal Neely's Star-Day company, and Neely launched Star-day King label. At the same time, he sold the James Brown masters to Polydor, who later acquired Mercury, where Brown had recorded with his orchestra, and brought the full Brown catalogue under one umbrella.

Star-day King was bought by legendary songwriters Leiber and Stoller in 1970, but the label was soon sold on again, this time to the Nashville-based label Gusto, which manages and re-issues original King recordings.

The pallbearers at King's funeral included former employee and Sire Records founder Seymour Stein, long-time King artist Hank Ballard and James Brown, who (so the story goes) acquired Nathan's old desk and added a new marble top which bore the inscription: 'I'll Always Remember The Man S Nathan'.

KING RECORDS

KING (JAPAN)

ESTABLISHED IN 1931 AS THE RECORD DIVISION OF JAPAN'S LARGEST MUSIC PUBLISHING HOUSE, Kodansha, King Records boasts its own recording studios and a host of best-selling Japanese pop, rock and jazz artists, such as Two-Mia, Miko Nakayama and Yuki Uchida. However, major success has come from the Evangelion animated movies and TV series, which has netted nearly six million record sales. Like other Japanese companies, it has decided to expand into Taiwan, where there is a growing market for J-pop. Rated among the world's top ten independents, King have added rock band Snail Ramp and singer Hideaki Tokunaga to their roster.

KOCH INTERNATIONAL

AUSTRIAN FRANZ KOCH FOUNDED THE COMPANY KOCH INTERNATIONAL IN 1975, and it now operates as a major distributor for German-language music throughout the world, including in America and India. It is also the largest producer of German folk music. Local acts such as Kastelruther Spatzen, Frans Bauer, Brunner And Brunner and million-selling violinist Andre Rieu are at the forefront of Koch's roster of acts, and their records are released around the world via Koch's network of more than 25 companies.

In 1987, Michael Koch (son of founder Franz) launched Koch in America, where it is established as Koch Entertainment. Alongside success from the company's franchise deals with the World Wrestling Federation (WWF) and Pokémon, Koch acquired Velvel Records, linked with the Artemis label, launched its own Koch Records (home to Ringo Starr and Carole King), as well as country imprint Audium (featuring Loretta Lynne and Charlie Daniels) and rap outlet In The Point.

KENT – see Modern

KEYNOTE – see Fantasy

US No 1
Singles **8**
Albums **2**

UK No 1
Singles **1**
Albums -

L

LAFACE

SUCCESSFUL MILLION-SELLING PRODUCERS AND SONGWRITERS ANTONIO REID AND KENNETH EDMONDS MOVED UP TO THE NEXT STAGE OF BUSINESS IN 1989 WHEN THEY CREATED LAFACE RECORDS, in a joint venture with BMG/Arista Records, using their own nicknames – LA Reid and Babyface Edmonds – to form the company name. Based in Atlanta, one of LaFace's earliest signings was Jermaine Jackson, but the label's first major success came with girl trio TLC and singer Toni Braxton, whose 1993 début album sold over nine million copies. In the same year, Reid and Edmonds, the label's co-presidents, ended their hit-making production partnership to focus on running the record company. Interviewed about his label, Reid once stated: 'I loved being a producer but I wanted to be more involved. I didn't want to just make a record and walk away. I wanted to be involved in every aspect, so we started LaFace.'

Concentrating on new black talent, LaFace went on to bolster its roster significantly with Usher, The Tony Rich Project and OutKast, the label's first rap act. The label celebrated its tenth anniversary in 1999 with its new signings Dru Hill, Goodie Mob and Shanice, while TLC went on to establish themselves as America's all-time best-selling female artists. Since then, BMG acquired the remaining share of the company owned by co-founders Reid and Edmonds and integrated the label with Arista – now run by Reid.

LAVA

LAVA RECORDS WAS FOUNDED IN 1995 BY JASON FLOM, who took on the role of President of his new label while remaining Senior Vice President of Atlantic Records where, after starting as a field sales rep in 1979, he signed Twisted Sister, Tori Amos and Clannad.

Lava was established within Atlantic Records and released its début album from Jill Sobule in 1995, followed by multi-million sellers Matchbox 20, Sugar Ray, Kid Rock and The Corrs (in conjunction with 143 Records).

It was reported that Flom sold his share of Lava to Atlantic for $50 million in 2001 but remained in charge of the label and its roster of 20+ artists, including Uncle Kracker and Cherie, whilst also performing as a stand-up comic at music industry charity events.

LEGACY

SONY MUSIC SET UP LEGACY RECORDINGS IN 1990 to restore and release the 100+-year-old catalogue housed in the Sony archive. The labels covered by Legacy's brief include the frontline Columbia and Epic imprints, plus the historic ARC, Okeh, Brunswick, Ode and Vocalion labels.

The recordings issued on Legacy from Sony's century-old catalogue feature artists such as Robert Johnson, Bessie Smith, Frank Sinatra, Miles Davis, Bob Dylan, Willie Nelson, Simon And Garfunkel and The Clash.

No 1
Singles **6**
Albums **5**

No 1
Singles **1**
Albums **1**

LIBERTY

THE TRIO OF CALIFORNIAN BUSINESSMEN WHO FOUNDED LIBERTY RECORDS IN 1955 WERE IMMORTALISED IN ONE OF THE LABEL'S MOST SUCCESSFUL ACTS. Alvin, Simon and Theodore from the novelty band The Chipmunks were actually named after label owners Al Bennett, Sy Waronker and Ted Keep by creator David Seville.

As early as 1957, the Pacific jazz label was acquired by Liberty, whose first successes featured Teresa Brewer and the aforementioned chart-topping band The Chipmunks before Eddie Cochran took Liberty into the rock 'n' roll era. He was closely followed by Johnny Burnette, Bobby Vee and soul singer Gene McDaniels, while the addition of the Imperial label in 1963 brought Fats Domino and Ricky Nelson to the Liberty stable. Further additions included the famous jazz label Blue Note, plus surf act Jan And Dean and blues group Canned Heat, after which Liberty was bought by United Artists in 1969. The label's roster of artists was merged alongside UA's hugely successful movie soundtrack releases and established acts such as Bobby Goldsboro, Jay And The Americans, The Crystals and Don McLean.

Following EMI Music's purchase of UA in 1979, the Liberty label faded into the background, although it re-emerged in the '90s as one of Capitol Records' country labels, and for a time its roster featured top-selling country superstar Garth Brooks.

No 1
Singles -
Albums -

No 1
Singles -
Albums **1**

LOADED/SKINT

BRIGHTON IS HOME TO BOTH THE LOADED AND SKINT LABELS, which have become firmly established among the UK's leading dance labels.

In 1990, Tim Jeffries and JC Reid formed the house label Loaded, which became home to hit acts Pizzaman, Impulsion and Wildchild. While Loaded took a break in the mid '90s, Skint was launched as an offshoot in 1995, and under the direction of Damien Harris the label launched Fatboy Slim (who was also Pizzaman, in addition to being former Housemartin Norman Cook), who rose to million-selling prominence with his 1999 album *You've Come A Long Way Baby*.

Skint continued to attract alternative dance talent, signing Lo-Fidelity Allstars and Space Raiders, as Loaded geared up and returned to business at the end of the '90s. Super Collider, Bert Dunk and Hakan were added to the roster while the teamed up with Glasgow's popular Sub club to release the compilation album Subversion.

LONDON

THE PRESTIGIOUS LONDON LABEL, WHICH IS NOW HOME TO BEST-SELLING ALL-GIRL GROUP ALL SAINTS, dates back to 1947, when it was founded as an imprint of Decca in America and served as an outlet for the company's UK artists. The UK counterpart of the label was set up two years later, successfully managing US stars such as Teresa Brewer, while in America the London label boasted the first US Number One single by a British group – 'Telstar', by the Tornadoes, in 1962 – and issued The Rolling Stones' major releases until 1969.

In the UK, the London label became home to a wide range of major American stars when US labels such as Imperial, Chess, Dot, Atlantic, Speciality and Sun licensed their recordings to Decca for release in the UK on London. Fats Domino, Little Richard, Chuck Berry, Jerry Lee Lewis and The Everly Brothers were among the acts who made early UK chart appearances on the London label.

The '60s brought more licensed deals to the UK London catalogue, with labels such as Big Top and Monument adding the artists Del Shannon and Roy Orbison. London also took on Phil Spector's Philles label, along with the host of hit artists that were signed directly to Decca. When these labels slowly began to move away from Decca, the London label suffered a major downturn in business. The last remaining successful label was Memphis-based Hi Records, whose star acts Al Green and Anne Peebles kept the London name in the UK charts in the early part of the '70s.

However, as the mighty Decca company floundered, so too did the London imprint, and following the death of Decca's

No 1
Singles **7**
Albums **2**

No 1
Singles **34**
Albums **4**

LONDON

founder, Sir Edward Lewis, in 1979 the company was acquired by Polygram. They eventually established a new look, re-launching the label as the independent-styled London Recordings in 1981, and acts such as New Edition, Blancmange, Bronski Beat, The Communards, Fine Young Cannibals and Bananarama took the London name back into the charts in the UK and the US.

In recent years Salt 'n' Pepa, Shakespear's Sister, The Brand New Heavies, Faith No More and Orbital turned London into an attractive operation, alongside subsidiary labels such Slash, Essential and FFRR (named after Decca's development of Full Frequency Range Recordings in the '60s). Following the Universal Music Group's acquisition of Polygram, outside the USA the London label was bought by the international arm of the Warner Music Group, who linked the label with the WEA division of Warner Music UK in 2001 and issued re-formed New Order, Australian chart topper Holly Valance and Dannii Minogue.

LUKE

FLORIDA-BORN LUTHER CAMPBELL WAS THE FRONTMAN OF RAP ACT 2 LIVE CREW when they earned the distinction of becoming the first group to have one of their records – 'As Nasty As They Wanna Be' – declared obscene, and thereby banned from being available to minors. Campbell changed his name to Luke Skywalker and launched his band on Luke Skywalker Records before film producer/director George Lucas threatened legal action against Campbell's use of the name Skywalker in 1990. Following this, the artist Luke and the label Luke Records were established.

Apart from being a member of 2 Live Crew, who were embroiled in an all-American controversy over censorship, Luke established his label as a home to emerging R&B and soul acts. However, Luke Records lost some impetus after 2 Live Crew split in 1993, and after a number of lawsuits, but under Campbell's continuing control the label forged new links with Loud Records.

LEADER – see Kapp

LOCKED ON – see Beggars Banquet Group

LOGO – see Transatlantic

LOUD – see Columbia

LYRIC – see Hollywood

Throughout his 25-year career, Sting has enjoyed a multitude of hits on A&M

The Supremes began the Motown label's dominance of the 1960s

Gareth Gates and Will Young served up an historic UK Number One on RCA

The Beach Boys: Capitol's surfin' stars

Manfred Mann had a string of '60s hits on HMV

Jerry Lee Lewis was part of Sun's million-dollar stable of artists

Robbie Williams flies a different Chrysalis flag nowadays

The Soul Man himself, Otis Redding: from valet to superstar on Stax

Destiny's Child enjoyed pre-Beyonce hits on Columbia

Isaac Hayes started out as a Stax staff musician before hitting the big time

Shania Twain keeps Mercury rising with her particular brand of country

Bruce Springsteen: the Boss still rules on Columbia

Led Zeppelin: from Atlantic to Swan Song and back again

The Eagles flew from Asylum to Elektra and watched the dollars pour in

The Beatles enjoyed a plethora of hits on Parlophone from 1962 until their break-up

The Corrs: credited to 143, Lava and Atlantic

U2 have had two decades of Island hits with their ever-innovative approach

The Spice Girls: five years of girl power with Virgin Records

Bob Marley, a legend on Island

Elvis Presley began his career with a handful of Sun singles

Justin Timberlake has triumphed with group and solo success on Jive

Britney Spears, the First Lady of Jive

Jethro Tull, the original Chrysalis superstars

Kylie Minogue, Parlophone's dance diva

Pink Floyd reaped their hits on Harvest

Garth Brooks: 90 million albums sold for Capitol and still counting!

Sarah Brightman, a classic HMV star

Missy Elliott has carried the Elektra torch into the 21st century

Marvin Gaye was one of the stalwarts of the Motown label

No 1
Singles -
Albums -

No 1
Singles 2
Albums -

M A G N E T

MAGNET

THE MAN NOW KNOWN FAMOUSLY AS LABOUR LIFE PEER LORD LEVY BEGAN MAGNET RECORDS IN THE EARLY '70S, when he was simply Michael Levy. Alvin Stardust started the ball rolling for Magnet in 1973, and he was closely followed by The Buzzcocks and then by Darts and Chris Rea, who charted on the Magnet label for over ten years, attracting a successful bid from the Warner Music International operation in 1988.

Rea went on to switch labels after the Magnet label was absorbed into Warner Music UK's operations, and Magnet's only further significant success in the '90s was with D:Ream's hit 'Things Can Only Get Better', which was adopted by the Labour party in Britain as their theme song.

MAJOR MINOR

PHIL SOLOMON, MANAGER OF THE BELFAST GROUP THEM (who featured Van Morrison), moved to England and started Major Minor Records in 1966 while at the same time investing in the pirate radio station Radio Caroline. Operating out of offices rented from DJM Records' boss Dick James, the label's first chart success came a year later courtesy of The Dubliners, and for the next two years Major Minor notched up hits with the American group Tommy James And The Shondells, Johnny Nash, Crazy Elephant and Karen Young.

Solomon's decision to pick up the banned single 'Je T'Aime...Moi Non Plus' by Jane Birkin and Serge Gainsbourg, after Fontana disowned the record, brought Major Minor a Number One hit and a glut of headlines. Major Minor's recordings were all released through Decca, but the catalogue was ultimately acquired by EMI.

No 1
Singles **1**
Albums **-**

No 1
Singles **3**
Albums **1**

MAM

WELSH SONGWRITER GORDON MILLS wrote Johnny Kidd's 1963 hit 'I'll Never Get Over You' before discovering singer Tom Jones and co-writing his first hit, 'It's Not Unusual'. He originally set up the MAM management company to look after Jones and fellow Decca act Engelbert Humperdinck.

The MAM record label followed in 1970 and blossomed, thanks to the unique skills and dress sense of Gilbert O'Sullivan – who racked up hits for a further five years – and Dave Edmunds' Number One hit 'I Hear You Knocking'. MAM's fortunes began to wane when Jones and Humperdinck moved to another management company, and in 1982 O'Sullivan successfully sued Mills for unpaid royalties. The MAM record label was eventually sold to Chrysalis by Mills, who died in 1986 at the age of only 51.

MATADOR

CHRIS LOMBARDI ESTABLISHED MATADOR RECORDS IN NEW YORK IN 1989 AND INITIALLY RAN THE BUSINESS OUT OF HIS APARTMENT.

His first signings, Austrian duo HP Zinker, were joined by Dustdevils and Superchunk before Gerard Cosloy joined the company in 1990 as co-owner. Scottish band Teenage Fanclub were added to the roster alongside Japan's Pizzicato Fuse, while American successes included Pavement, Liz Phair and The Jon Spencer Blues Explosion.

In 1996, Matador opened offices in the UK and in 2002 UK indie Beggars Banquet bought 50% of the company and took over international marketing, while Beggars Banquet US moved into Matador's New York offices.

No 1
Singles **2**
Albums **6**

No 1
Singles **3**
Albums **4**

MAVERICK

IN 1992, AFTER EIGHT YEARS AS ONE OF THE WORLD'S BIGGEST SUPERSTARS, Madonna decided to launch her own commercial enterprise. In a joint venture with Warner Bros Records she set up a record label, along with book publishing, merchandising and movie divisions, which reportedly earned her $60 million.

The Maverick record label (the name comes from the first letters of the singer's names Madonna Veronica and the end of the christian name of her then manager, Frederick DeMann) boasted singer Me'shell Ndege'ocello and early grunge act Candlebox among its first signings, but it was in 1995 that the label made an real impact. Not only did Madonna switch to her own imprint in order to release the hit 'Take A Bow' but also a Canadian singer/songwriter named Alanis Morissette emerged with the album *Jagged Little Pill*, which became the biggest-selling début album by a female artist, with sales in excess of 25 million.

Maverick Records is now established as a major player, particularly since UK dance act Prodigy and Erasure were added to its roster for America, and the label released the soundtrack of the hit movie *The Matrix*, which generated revenues in excess of $770 million. In 2002, both Madonna and Morissette brought Maverick's first decade to a close with Number One records as new signings The Deftones and Michelle Branch emerged.

M·C·A

MUSIC CORPORATION

⁽ᵒᶠ⁾ AMERICA

US No 1
Singles **28**
Albums **24**

UK No 1
Singles **6**
Albums **5**

MCA

THE MUSIC CORPORATION OF AMERICA WAS FOUNDED BY JULES STERN IN 1924 AS A BOOKING AGENCY BEFORE THE COMPANY MOVED INTO MANAGEMENT, music publishing and the film business with the legendary Universal Studios. The first MCA music operation was started in 1962 with the purchase of Decca USA and the rights to early Brunswick and Vocalion recordings, along with major artists such as Louis Armstrong, Bing Crosby and Duke Ellington. More recently-acquired labels – such as Coral, Brunswick, ABC, ABC-Paramount, Chess, Impulse, Dot and Dunhill, plus the '60s in-house subsidiary label UNI – were all assembled under the MCA group name, while the company finally severed its links with Decca in 1974 by switching its UK licensing deal to EMI.

During the '70s, MCA boasted a large roster of artists, such as Lynyrd Skynyrd, Neil Diamond, Tony Christie and Osibisa, plus the successful Tim Rice/Andrew Lloyd Webber musicals *Jesus Christ, Superstar* and *Evita*. Olivia Newton-John, Elton John (both signed for the US only), Rose Royce and Tiffany also served to enhance the image of the MCA label, which later launched its own international operations and succeeded through the '80s with the likes of Kim Wilde, Musical Youth, Tom Petty and Meat Loaf (in the US only).

In 1989, MCA acquired Geffen Records and the services of its founder, David Geffen, on the subsidiary label DGC, along with acts Guns N' Roses and Nirvana, and a year later the Japanese corporation Matushita acquired the MCA company.

In the same year, MCA added the prestigious jazz label GRP and linked with the Radioactive, Uptown and Curb labels. Meanwhile, the MCA Nashville division dominated the American country and western charts, thanks to label acts Vince Gill, Reba McIntire, The Mavericks, Nanci Griffith and Trisha Yearwood, as well as catalogues featuring Patsy Cline, Loretta Lynn and George Jones.

In 1996, the Canadian Seagrams corporation purchased MCA for a reported $5.7 billion and created the Universal Music Group, while maintaining the MCA name as a separate record label. MCA retained its chart presence thanks to Bobby Brown, Mary J Blige, Shaggy and Blink 182 but, in 2003, became part of Universal's Interscope/Geffen/A&M division.

No 1
Singles **20**
Albums **11**

No 1
Singles **11**
Albums **21**

MERCURY

HOME TO MILLION-SELLING US SUPERSTAR SHANIA TWAIN AND TOP BRITISH BAND TEXAS, Mercury Records was conceived in Chicago in 1947 by Irving Green, Berle Adams and Art Talmadge. The company launched both pressing and distribution operations and grew quickly, and within a year Mercury enjoyed its first hits (from Frankie Laine) and added the Majestic label to its ranks. In the late '50s and early '60s, Mercury began to enter the charts regularly, thanks to The Platters, Johnny Preston, The Big Bopper (who died in an air crash in 1959, along with Buddy Holly) and Bruce Channel, a star of the Smash label, which Mercury bought out in 1962.

Quincy Jones was one of Mercury's early staff producers, and while he was working on Lesley Gore's 1963 hit 'It's My Party' the company was being acquired by the Dutch company Philips. This led to Mercury becoming established as the Polygram Music Group's main US label, while in the UK it operated as the premier pop/rock label within the Phonogram division.

Active in the pop and rock genres in the '70s, Mercury brought fame to Rod Stewart, Bachman-Turner Overdrive, Spirit and 10cc, who were originally signed to Jonathan King's UK label in 1972. The label moved smoothly into the next decade with Dexy's Midnight Runners and Tears For Fears.

In the '90s, the decision was taken to change the name of the division from Phonogram (which was only a corporate identity and never actually a label) to the more appropriate Mercury Records, which incorporated the Fontana, Vertigo and Rocket labels along with the personal imprints of Wet Wet Wet (Precious) and Bon Jovi (Jambco).

While multi-million seller Shania Twain and Texas topped the Mercury roster at the end of the '90s, the label's dance imprint Manifesto and Talkin' Loud division, along with the emerging Serious imprint, achieved success for the label that, as part of Universal Music, is linked with the Island and Def Jam operations. UK TV talent-show entrants Darius and David Sneddon became Mercury chart toppers in the UK, while the soundtrack to the film *O Brother, Where Art Thou?* became a multi-milion selling US Number One album.

METAL BLADE

BRIAN SLAGEL FOUNDED METAL BLADE RECORDS IN LOS ANGELES IN 1982 ON THE BACK OF HIS INTEREST IN BRITISH HEAVY METAL BANDS SUCH AS IRON MAIDEN AND SAXON.

A college student who worked part-time in a record store, Slagel decided to create an LA-based heavy-metal compilation album entitled *Metal Massacre*, featuring then-unknown local band Metallica. With money borrowed from family and friends, Slagel launched Metal Blade Records with the *Metal Massacre* title as its first release and soon added bands Bitch and Warlord to the roster.

By 1985, Slagel – with three Massacre compilations under his belt and in the stores – opened his first office and hired staff. Distribution through Warner Bros Records ensured more success and resulted in the signing of The Goo Goo Dolls who, however, remained with Warner Bros when the distribution deal ended.

New acts such as Armored Saint and Spook's Beard joined the roster alongside the Radiant, Magic Circle and Prosthetic imprints. Twenty years on, Slagel remains at the head of Metal Blade, which boasts a roster of more than 50 artists.

No 1
Singles **16**
Albums **3**

No 1
Singles **11**
Albums -

MGM

MGM RECORDS WAS FORMED AS A DIVISION OF THE HIGHLY SUCCESSFUL MGM FILM COMPANY IN 1946 FOR THE PURPOSE OF EXPLOITING THE STUDIO'S FILM SCORES. On the heels of C&W star Hank Williams and jazz singer Billy Eckstine, MGM Records initiated a rock roster in the late '50s with the likes of Tommy Edwards, Conway Twitty and Sheb Wooley, whose 'The Purple People Eater' was the first US Number One for MGM. Later, Connie Francis was also signed.

After opening the subsidiary label Cub, MGM's success in the '60s came mainly from British groups, including The Animals. Producer Mickie Most recalls how the band ended up at MGM: 'Representatives from MGM were visiting EMI in England and asking how come they hadn't got The Beatles or any other Mersey acts. Len Wood, head of EMI, who distributed MGM in the UK, looked through the charts, saw the record by The Animals and said "You can have The Animals for America," and that's how MGM got them.' The Animals and Herman's Hermits both hit Number One in America on MGM, who built on their range of artists by expanding the Verve label from its jazz origins and adding the likes of Tim Hardin, Laura Nyro, Richie Havens and The Velvet Underground.

Under the direction of Mike Curb, MGM went on to land The Osmonds, who hit the charts during the early '70s as a group, and the label also released the solo offerings of Donny, Jimmy and Marie. By the middle of the decade, MGM had been acquired by Polydor. CW McCall's famous 1975 CB track 'Convoy' was the last major pop hit on the MGM label. Under new ownership, MGM reverted to being used for soundtrack releases and remains one of the many imprints owned by the Universal Music Group, following their acquisition of Polygram.

MILAN

AMONG THE WORLD'S FOREMOST SOUNDTRACK COMPANIES, Milan Records was founded in France by Emmanuel Chamboredon in 1977.

Based in Paris, with offices in California, Milan has specialised in soundtrack recordings and boasts music from films including *Backdraft*, *Brazil*, *Little Buddha* and *Mulholland Drive*, alongside composers and performers such as Maurice Jarre, Ennio Morricone and Angelo Badalmenti.

Sister label Jade releases liturgical music, while Milan also offers jazz and electronic titles including the renowned 'Man Ray' series.

MINISTRY OF SOUND

MINISTRY OF SOUND HAS BEEN ONE OF THE SUCCESS STORIES OF THE UK MUSIC BUSINESS SINCE ITS FORMATION IN 1993 AS A DANCE COMPILATION LABEL FOLLOWING THE COMPANY'S INITIAL SUCCESS AS A LONDON NIGHTCLUB. The label's first release in 1993 featured the club's initial resident DJ Tony Humphries, and led to a series of specialist dance album and single releases. In 1998, Ministry Of Sound notched up six Number Ones in the UK compilation chart, and the label's 'Annual' and 'Dance Nation' series – established by Pete Tong, Boy George and newcomers Tall Paul and Brandon Block – are established million-selling records.

In 1999, the new 'Clubber's Guide To...' and 'Trance Nation' titles were introduced, alongside MOS's first foray into A&R and artist development, which included links with the labels Defected, Incentive, Relentless and Azuli. The music arm of the label – which features the four wholly-owned subsidiary labels Sound Of Ministry, Ride, FSUK* and Data – boasts total sales of over ten million units, plus a roster which features Blockster, ATB and Baby Bumps.

Internationally linked with a number of major record companies, the MOS music division sat alongside merchandising, promotion, publishing, club touring and radio production as part of the multi-million pound MOS industry until business took a downturn in 2002.

Following venture capital firm 3I's acquisition of 15% of the company for £24 million, founder James Palumbo stepped down as chief executive. The UK's leading independent closed both its magazine and joint-venture label Relentless but added new artists such as Romeo and Fischerspooner to the MOS roster.

Modern

No 1
Singles -
Albums **1**

No 1
Singles -
Albums -

MODERN

BROTHERS JULES, SAUL, LESTER AND JOE BIDHARI
were the founders of Modern Records in LA in 1945 and
oversaw its growth into one of the great R&B labels. With an
impressive distribution operation and its own pressing plant,
Modern was able to ensure nationwide awareness for its roster,
including the signing of Etta James, John Lee Hooker and
Lightnin' Hopkins. In the early '50s, the brothers set up a
number of subsidiary labels, which included RPM, Flair and
Meteor, and recorded the music of important artists, such as
BB King, Johnny 'Guitar' Watson and Elmore James. One the
label's talent scouts was Ike Turner.

Modern's range of labels soon featured a host of R&B and
blues legends, including Howlin' Wolf, Junior Parker and Jimmy
Witherspoon. With the emergence of new independent labels
in the late '50s, the Bihari brothers formed Crown Records
and Kent Records, focusing their attention on releasing budget
recordings. However, the whole Modern empire came to a full
stop following the death of Jules Bihari, although its important
back catalogue is available on specialist labels.

No 1
Singles **3**
Albums **1**

No 1
Singles -
Albums -

MONUMENT

THE NASHVILLE-BASED LABEL MONUMENT RECORDS WAS SET UP IN 1958 BY FORMER ABC PARAMOUNT STAFFER FRED FOSTER WITH A BUDGET OF $1,200. One of the label's first signings was former Sun Records artist Roy Orbison, who had hit records with Monument until 1965. Foster produced records and even wrote sleeve notes for his Monument releases, and he issued the memorable single 'The Shag Is Totally Cool' in the late '50s to capitalise on the dance craze of the title.

The label was named after the famous Washington Monument, and its rosters boasted the likes of Dolly Parton, Joe Simon, Willie Nelson, Kris Kristofferson, Boots Randolph and Billy Swan, who took Monument back to the top of the US charts in 1974. Monument was bought by CBS in 1986, and after it lay dormant for a decade the label was reactivated in the late '90s, becoming home to award-winning all-girl country-rock band The Dixie Chicks.

MOONSHINE

BRITISH BROTHERS STEVE AND JON LEVY CREATED
MOONSHINE IN LOS ANGELES IN 1992 and have overseen
its growth into one of America's leading independent dance/
electronic labels.

Founded around the concept of DJ-mixed compilations
including Judge Jules and Bill Nasty, Moonshine, which was
the name of the brothers' early illegal warehouse-party
operation, expanded with touring DJs – their annual Moonshine
Overamerica tour ran from 1997 to 2000 – and now features
artists including Cirrus, Tall Paul, Mistress Barbara and Gusgus.

Distributed by Koch, Moonshine added a vinyl-only label,
Moonshine RGB (red for house and techno/green for
breakbeat/blue for trance), in 2001, closely followed by the
Moonshine Movies division.

MOTOWN

THE LABEL THAT, ACCORDING TO FOUNDER BERRY GORDY, WAS 'BORN' RATHER THAN FOUNDED began its journey to the forefront of American black music in 1959 when ex-boxer and former record store owner Gordy was given an $800 loan by a family co-operative. Forty years later, and despite being under the control of three different owners since 1988, Motown – which was the birthplace of acts ranging from Marvin Gaye and The Supremes to The Jackson 5 and Boyz II Men – remains a name that represents emerging black talent in America.

Gordy, who also worked on the assembly line at the local Ford car plant, experienced success as a songwriter (he wrote 'Reet Petite' for Jackie Wilson) and as a recording artist, with the chart hit 'Money (That's What I Want)', before starting up his own record label. He named his label after his home town of Detroit, which was known as Motor City, and an early influence on him was Smokey Robinson, who persuaded him to manufacture and distribute his own records. Robinson wrote and recorded the company's first million-selling record, 'Shop Around', for the Tamla label in 1961, and has been quoted as saying: 'Motown started very precariously. Berry was the first black trying to break into the record business, and for many years we struggled. We would mail out the records, take them to the shops and radio stations, but we loved what we were doing.' In his autobiography, *To Be Loved*, Gordy wrote that his original plan was for all solo artists to appear on Tamla and all groups to be released on Motown. 'Each label would have its own image and identity – solo artists versus groups. But this plan, like some others, turned out not to be practical.'

In 1962, a new Gordy label was introduced, named after the founder's family. Looking back on his first years in business, Gordy says: 'Having been around a lot of the crowd coming from the ghetto, and the blues-loving people, we really dug the type of things that reflected the society. I felt that this was something that could be a very good force in American music.'

The music of Motown was christened 'the sound of young America', and the label went on to deliver artists such as Marvin Gaye, Martha Reeves, The Supremes, The Four Tops, The Temptations and Stevie Wonder onto the world stage. From its earliest

MOTOWN

days, supported only by Gordy's original loan, Motown had had strong 'family' ties. Martha Reeves and Diana Ross, who lived on the same street as Smokey Robinson, both started at the company as secretaries before their emergence as pop stars. 'I was making five dollars a night singing when I was asked to go into Motown,' recalled Reeves in Joe Smith's *Off The Record*. 'I went into work next morning at nine o'clock and became Motown's first A&R secretary.'

Motown notched up its first American Number One single in 1964, with Mary Wells' 'My Guy'. In the same year, the company sold three million albums and twelve million singles, and released ten per cent of America's Top 100 hits. In addition to signing artists, Gordy also turned his attention to working with writers and producers, and formed in-house teams including Holland/Dozier/Holland, Whitfield and Strong, and Ashford and Simpson.

The closeness of the Motown 'family' was further illustrated by the fact that The Supremes performed backing vocals for Marvin Gaye, and that Smokey Robinson – who was later to become a senior executive with the label – wrote, arranged and produced for other artists. Diana Ross also brought The Jackson 5 to the label, and Gordy's own educational programme at the Michigan State School For The Blind resulted in him discovering Stevie Wonder.

While Motown, Gordy and Tamla (the name for which was taken from Debbie Reynolds' hit 'Tammy' but was changed for registration reasons) existed as separate labels in America, on an international level the company adopted a simpler imprint. The unified Tamla Motown label become home to numerous hits in the UK and around the world for over 20 years, many of them introduced to the British public by The Beatles, who were early fans of the Motown sound.

In 1971, Gordy moved his company from the famous address at 2648 West Grand Boulevard, Detroit (where the words 'Hitsville USA' were hung over the door), to Los Angeles. However, as he entered the movie business with titles such *Lady Sings The Blues*, established Motown stars such as Diana Ross, Marvin Gaye, The Jacksons and Gladys Knight began to leave the label. In the '80s, the label that had

No 1
Singles **37**
Albums **11**

No 1
Singles **11**
Albums **10**

MOTOWN

briefly entertained the idea of developing a roster of white artists, launching the short-lived Rare Earth label, proved to be a label in decline despite enjoying hits from The Commodores, Lionel Richie, Teena Marie and Rick James.

In 1988 Gordy decided to sell the Motown record operation to MCA for a reported $61 million, while he retained the lucrative publishing arm, Jobete, for a further year. The founder and owner of Motown has detailed in print his final days in charge of the label: 'One afternoon in 1988 Smokey Robinson ambled in and said he wanted to get a smash hit right now more than ever. I told him that he needed a whole lot more than a couple of smashes. The only way I could save the company now was to sell.'

While the emergence of the group Boyz II Men in the early '90s brought renewed presence for Motown, in 1993 MCA still sold the company to Polygram, who operated the label until the Seagrams corporation purchased Polygram in 1999, linking it with their own Universal label to create the Universal/Motown Records Group. New artists such as Brian McKnight, India.Arie and Remy Shand have ensured that the name Motown has rarely been absent from the charts in more than four decades.

MUSHROOM

No 1
Singles -
Albums -

No 1
Singles 2
Albums 4

MUSHROOM

THE AUSTRALIAN INDEPENDENT RECORD LABEL THAT LAUNCHED
KYLIE MINOGUE and Peter Andre on the road to international success was founded
in Melbourne by 20 year old Michael Gudinski in 1972. Credited as being the man
who created the independent record industry in Australia, Gudinski first tasted success
with local act Skyhooks. He then went on to sign Split Enz and Jimmy Barnes, and
formed Liberation Records as an outlet for product licensed from UK and US labels
such as Mute, Tommy Boy and Jive.

Grudinski is on record as saying that 'The Australian industry was seen to be
second rate, and I saw that I had to pull together and do it myself.' He went on to
sign The Saints, and in the late '80s he added TV soap stars Kylie Minogue and Jason
Donovan to his label, releasing their music – including their UK chart hits –
internationally through PWL.

In 1993, Gudinski sold 49% of Mushroom Records to Rupert Murdoch's News
Corporation and used the funds to establish overseas operations, including Mushroom
UK. Within a year, the best-selling group Garbage were signed to the label, and they
were followed by Pop Will Eat Itself and Ash, who appeared on the new British joint
venture label Infectious Records. Following Garbage's global success, Mushroom
finally achieved its first UK Number One hit with Peter Andre in 1996.

The News Corporation – which acquired the long-standing Australian label Festival
Records in the '60s and launched the US rap label Rawkus in 1994 – acquired the
outstanding 51% of Mushroom Records for a reported $25.6 million in 1998,
expanding the company's music and new media division, which was run by James
Murdoch. A year later the Mushroom and Festival companies merged in Australia,
while former owner Gudinski – who retained the name Mushroom – launched a new
Mushroom marketing/record company and re-launched the Liberation label. After
selling their US label Rawkus, News Corp also oversaw the sale of Mushroom Records
UK to Warner Music UK in 2003.

No 1
Singles -
Albums -

No 1
Singles 1
Albums 11

MUTE

IN 1978, RECORD PRODUCER DANIEL MILLER – a former member of Silicon Teen – established his Mute label in West London as a home for electronic and hi-tech music. The label's first success came in 1981 with Depeche Mode, who were allegedly signed to Mute on a handshake deal which ran until a formal agreement was signed in 1986. Miller financed and produced the label's first Depeche Mode titles, and these were closely followed by ex-band member Vince Clarke's projects Yazoo and Erasure.

Financed by the continuing success of both Depeche Mode and Erasure, Mute launched a host of credible but not-entirely-commercial artists. Acquiring the back catalogues of Cabaret Voltaire and Can further enhanced the status of the label, which also launched the 13th Hour subsidiary and the techno label Novamute, which became the international home for New York dance star Moby.

After two decades in the business, the signing and success of Inspiral Carpets (together with their own Cow imprint) and Nick Cave, alongside Depeche Mode's continuing loyalty to the label, ensured Mute's position as a small but successful UK independent company. However, that situation changed early in 2002 when Miller sold Mute to EMI Music for £24 million. Despite the sale, he remained in charge, stressing that Mute 'maintains creative control of everything that we do'.

MAJESTIC – see Mercury

MALA – see Bell

MAMMOTH – see Hollywood

MANGO – see Island

MANHATTAN – see Blue Note/Capitol/Chrysalis

MANIFESTO – see Mercury

MANTICORE – see Island

MANTRA – see Beggars Banquet Group

MARLIN – see TK

MEDIARTS – see United Artists

MELEE – see Dreamworks

METAL IS – see Sanctuary

METEOR – see Modern

MINIT – see Imperial

MOJO – see Universal

MOONGLOW – see Philles

MO'WAX – see Beggars Banquet Group

MULTIPLY – see Telstar

MYRR – see Word Entertainment

NAXOS

NAXOS, ESTABLISHED IN HONG KONG IN 1987, has grown over the years to become the world's leading classical-music label, with a catalogue of over 25,000 albums.

Naxos was created by founder Klaus Heymann as an offshoot of HNH International, Asia's largest record distributor, in order to meet the demand in the Far East for low-priced classical CDs.

Originally, Naxos recordings were made in Slovakia and Hungary, but by 1994 new recordings and artists were added from Western Europe and America. Alongside Maria Kliegel and Jeno Jando, Naxos added contemporary composers Henryck Górecki, Philip Glass, Michael Nyman and John Tavener.

No 1
Singles **1**
Albums -

No 1
Singles -
Albums -

NEIGHBORHOOD

WHEN NEW YORK-BORN FOLK SINGER MELANIE
FELL OUT WITH BUDDAH RECORDS IN 1971, she started
up her own label, Neighborhood Records, with her manager
husband Peter Schekeryk, and immediately hit the top of the
charts with 'Brand New Key'. Melanie recorded for her own
label for the next four years, and the label also took on few
other unsuccessful signings before being closed in 1975 and
sold to the growing MCA corporation.

No 1
Singles -
Albums **4**

No 1
Singles -
Albums -

NO LIMIT

IN 1990, RAPPER MASTER P launched his own recording career from his record shop in California before moving on to start up No Limit Records in 1992. Born Percy Miller, Master P claims that the label is 'the largest independent hip-hop label in the world', and in addition to his own successful albums No Limit also boasts a roster which includes Snoop Dogg, Tru and Mystikal among its best-selling artists. The label has been distributed through Priority since 1995, and Master P has also taken No Limit into the movie business, with titles such as *I Got The Hook-Up*.

With over 20 top-selling albums to its name, No Limit has helped to establish Master P – who boasts of retaining all of the rights to his label's recordings – among America's most successful businessmen. He held a place in the Top Ten of the *Forbes* magazine's list of America's richest men.

NONESUCH

NONESUCH

JAC HOLZMAN, WHO FOUNDED ELEKTRA RECORDS IN 1950, launched Nonesuch as a subsidiary label for budget classical releases. His initial releases were such things as a tribute to the Baroque trumpet, an anthology of obscure French composers, a Morse code tutorial and a sound-effects library. After the success of parent company Elektra through into the '80s, Nonesuch reappeared as a label for classical, contemporary, world and traditional American music with the likes of John Adams, Steve Reich and The Kronos Quartet. The label continued as a division of Elektra into the '90s, when, as part of the major Warner Music Group, it was moved to the London-based Warner Classics international division.

As well as being home to working acts such as Mandy Patinkin and The Gypsy Kings and also re-creating the musicals of George and Ira Gershwin, Nonesuch was responsible for releasing the biggest-selling classical record from a living composer with the 1992 release of Henryck Górecki's third symphony, featuring the soprano Dawn Upshaw. More recently Nonesuch switched to Warner Music Group's Atlantic Records and continued to produce highly respected recordings featuring Philip Glass, Buena Vista Social Club, Dawn Upshaw and Wilco.

No 1
Singles -
Albums -

No 1
Singles **3**
Albums -

nude

NUDE

SCOTSMAN SAUL GALPERN DID THE ROUNDS AS A&R MAN WITH THE MAJOR RECORD LABELS BEFORE HE SET UP NUDE RECORDS IN 1991, in his flat in northwest London. He launched the label with Suede, and in 1993 the band's début album topped the charts, opening the way for further Nude signings such as Sharkboy, Goya Dress and Geneva. Ex-Associates singer Billy MacKenzie's last album was released posthumously on Nude in 1997, and newer signings Ultrasound, Mainstream and Black Box Recorder fill the roster alongside stalwarts Suede.

Sadly, as the label neared its 10th anniversary, Nude Records went into voluntary liquidation leaving Suede linked with long-time label supporters Sony Music.

NEPTUNE – see Philadelphia International

NIXA – see Pye

NORTHWESTSIDE – see Arista

NOVAMUTE – see Mute

No 1
Singles **1**
Albums **3**

No 1
Singles -
Albums -

O

ODE

LOU ADLER WAS AMONG AMERICAN POP MUSIC'S LEADING ENTREPRENEURS FOR OVER TWO DECADES, and launched Ode Records in 1967 as one of his final music ventures before he moved into film and TV production.

Manager of surf act Jan And Dean, along with trumpeter and eventual A&M founder Herb Alpert, songwriter and producer Adler later moved to Ode after selling his Dunhill label to ABC. Scott McKenzie got the label under way with the hippie anthem 'San Francisco (Wear Some Flowers In Your Hair)' before Spirit and Carole King were added to the roster. Songwriter Carole King (the Carol in Neil Sedaka's hit 'Oh! Carol') also recorded her 1971 album *Tapestry* for Ode, with Adler as her manager and producer. The album spent 302 weeks in the US album chart, a record for a female solo artist.

Adler teamed up with Alpert again, signing a deal which would allow A&M to distribute the Ode label. However, as Adler moved away from music in the mid '70s in order to focus on new initiatives, the Ode recordings found different homes, with the CD of Carole King's Tapestry being released on Epic/Ode through Sony.

OKEH

THE AMERICAN LABEL OKEH RECORDS WAS SET UP IN 1918, and it has been credited as being responsible for releasing the first blues record made by a black artist. Among its earliest signings was singer Mamie Smith, whose 1920 record 'Crazy Blues' was certainly Okeh's first big hit. Later signings included King Oliver's Creole Jazz Band, Louis Armstrong and The Dorsey Brothers before Okeh became part of the American Columbia company, which used the label as an outlet for blues recordings by the likes of Brownie McGhee and Blind Willie McTell.

In the late '50s, it was used as a new pop/rock imprint for Johnny Ray, whose chart hit 'Cry' also became a major R&B record, largely because he was thought to be a black singer on the black Okeh label. In the '60s, however, Okeh enjoyed a whole new lease of life as it re-emerged as the home of soul singers Major Lance, Billy Butler, Larry Williams, Ted Taylor and Johnny Guitar Watson.

Despite never having made a sustained impression on the charts, Okeh's reputation was enhanced in the mid '90s when new blues star Keb' Mo's releases were issued on the label.

No 1
Singles -
Albums -

No 1
Singles 1
Albums -

ONE LITTLE INDIAN

DEREK BIRKETT WAS THE BASS PLAYER WITH '80s PUNK BAND FLUX OF PINK INDIANS AND ALSO RAN THEIR LABEL, SPIDERLEG. He eventually set up One Little Indian Records, whose first success came in 1988 with Icelandic group The Sugarcubes.

The label's success continued with the addition of dance act The Shamen and Kitchens Of Distinction in the early '90s, but the solo releases by former Sugarcubes singer Björk firmly established OIL as one of the UK's top indie labels. Chumbawamba and Skunk Anansie maintained the label's status, but their departure left Björk to fly the flag alongside Manchild and Manbreak.

One-time owners of early Rough Trade recordings, One Little Indian, still owned and operated by Birkett, signed a US distribution deal with Navarre Entertainment Media in 2003.

ORIOLE

ORIOLE WAS A UK INDEPENDENT LABEL WHICH WAS FOUNDED IN THE '50s. After the skiffle successes of Chas McDevitt and Nancy Whiskey, the label had a further decade of limited success with singer Maureen Evans and Swedish guitar group The Spotniks, who delivered UK chart hits between 1960 and 1964. For brief period, Oriole handled the releases of emerging US label Motown in the UK, but that label's move to EMI in 1963 ended the association. Oriole was eventually absorbed into the CBS operation in the mid '60s, and after that the label was rarely seen.

ODEON – see Columbia (EMI)

PABLO

TEN YEARS AFTER HE SOLD HIS JAZZ LABELS TO MGM, including the world-famous Verve imprint, Norman Granz started up Pablo Records in 1973. Initially featuring recordings by the acts that he managed, such as Ella Fitzgerald, Oscar Peterson and Joe Pass, Granz later added recordings by the likes of Count Basie, John Coltrane, Dizzy Gillespie and Sarah Vaughan to the catalogue. With a total of over 350 albums on the label, Pablo was sold by Granz in 1987 to Fantasy, who continue to release previously unissued recordings and add new jazz artists to the roster.

No 1
Singles **2**
Albums **1**

No 1
Singles -
Albums **3**

PAISLEY PARK

JUST OVER FIVE YEARS AFTER HE SIGNED HIS FIRST RECORD DEAL WITH WARNER BROS, Prince started up his own Paisley Park record label in 1984 as the imprint for his own recordings and a host of close musical friends. After chart success with albums such as 1999 and *Purple Rain*, the Minneapolis-based artist Prince Rogers Nelson launched the Paisley Park label with his album *Around The World In A Day*, and later added to the roster the band Time (featuring Morris Day), producers Jimmy Jam and Terry Lewis, backing singer Sheila E, and artists Mavis Staples and George Clinton.

While Prince has changed his identity (although he is now once more known as Prince) and moved between record labels, Paisley Park has dramatically reduced both its artists' roster and release schedule.

PARAMOUNT

A FURNITURE COMPANY FOUNDED IN ONE OF AMERICA'S NORTHERN STATES IN THE 1880s was the driving force behind the historic blues label Paramount Records.

Wisconsin Chair Factory produced cabinets for record players and launched Paramount Records in 1915 in order to boost their cabinet-making business.

With offices and studios in New York, Paramount launched itself as a 'race' label, with artists including Ma Rainey and King Oliver's Creole Jazz Band. After passing on blues legend Robert Johnson, the label signed Blind Lemon Jefferson in 1926, followed by Charles Patton and Tommy Johnston.

In 1932, Paramount closed down, abandoning its studio, and the master recordings that survived were re-released in the 1940s by SD Records. Paramount was revived briefly by Wisconsin Chair Factory in the late 1940s, focusing on jazz recordings, but the label finally closed its doors at the of the end of the 1950s.

TRADE   MARK

Parlophone

PARLOPHONE

PARLOPHONE JOINED THE LIST OF THE WORLD'S MOST FAMOUS
RECORD LABELS IN THE SWINGING '60s, when it became the home of the
world's most successful recording group of all time, The Beatles.

The company's origins, however, lie in Germany with the record manufacturer
Carl Lindstrom, who founded the label before the First World War. Parlophone – with
its familiar £ logo, which is said to have developed from the original trademark of a
German letter L – began life in the early '20s as a classical label. In 1927, the British
Columbia Graphophone company purchased Lindstrom's operations, including the
Dutch subsidiary Transoceanic Trading and the Parlophone label, with its famous R
prefix, which still featured on Parlophone single releases 70 years later.

After the Columbia buy-out, Parlophone was given repertoire from the American
jazz label Okeh and, as a result, early British releases by The Dorsey Brothers and
Louis Armstrong appeared on the label. The formation of EMI in 1931, following the
merger of Columbia and the Gramophone Company, meant that Parlophone then
found itself up alongside the more famous HMV and Columbia labels.

Among Parlophone's releases during the big band era of the '30s were records
by American stars Nat Gonella and Duke Ellington. These were joined by British artists
Leslie 'Hutch' Hutchinson and Victor Sylvester, who both later switched from
Parlophone to EMI sister labels, while Richard Tauber – an Austrian Jew who fled
from Germany in 1938 – continued as the only major act on Parlophone during World
War Two, which led to the label being dubbed 'Tauberphone'. After the war had ended,
Parlophone continued to struggle within EMI, but in 1950 a former student from the
Guildhall School Of Music was taken on to expand the label's roster of UK talent.
George Martin soon spotted the rivalry that existed between EMI's three labels: 'It
was intense, and HMV and Columbia were the chief protagonists while Parlophone
stayed on the sidelines because it was the weakest.'

The music of home-grown talent issued by Parlophone during the '50s included
that of The Frank Chacksfield Orchestra (whose 1953 hit 'Little Red Monkey' was
probably the label's first chart record), Jimmy Shand, Eve Boswell, Johnny Dankworth

PARLOPHONE

and Laurie London, who reached Number Two in America in 1957 with his UK hit 'He's Got The Whole World In His Hands'.

Following in the footsteps of original Parlophone manager Oscar Preus, who had recorded a host of music hall stars for the label, Martin added his own 'comic' releases. Dick James recorded the famous theme to the TV series *Robin Hood*, and hit the charts alongside Eamonn Andrews, Charlie Drake and Peter Sellers, who ultimately teamed up with Italian actress Sophia Loren to make the unlikely hits 'Goodness Gracious Me' and 'Bangers And Mash'.

These successes vindicated the faith shown in Martin and Parlophone by EMI Chairman Sir Joseph Lockwood, who supported the search for new British producers and talent. 'In the '50s Parlophone was nothing, but I encouraged Martin and his colleagues even though they only bought in a few odd bits each year.' Among those 'odd bits' were Parlophone's first Number One in 1957 (by Adam Faith) and Martin's own début Number One as a producer two years later, with The Temperance Seven. At this time, as head of Parlophone, Martin was earning the princely sum of £7 4s 3d per week, and he continued to add British talent in the shape of '60s successes Matt Monro, Bernard Cribbins and Mike Sarne, whose Number One hit 'Come Outside' featured future *EastEnders* star Wendy Richards.

In 1962, however, things took a new and dramatic turn for both Parlophone and George Martin in the shape of four young men from Liverpool. John Lennon, Paul McCartney, George Harrison and Ringo Starr had been turned down by both Decca and EMI before Martin met, heard and ultimately signed The Beatles to his label. With their success, Martin went on to sign more Merseyside acts from the stable of their manager, Brian Epstein. Cilla Black, Billy J Kramer And The Dakotas, The Fourmost and Gerry And The Pacemakers were all produced by Martin, who worked to a simple schedule: 'With The Beatles we aimed for a single every three months and an album twice a year. We would plan for a Beatles single in one month, which meant we could release a Gerry single [on Columbia] and a Cilla record in different months.'

Parlophone also became home to Manchester group The Hollies, while Cliff

PARLOPHONE

Bennett, Keith West and Scaffold continued the label's extraordinary run of hit records throughout the '60s. EMI's 'poor relation' became so successful that Parlophone R-series records topped the UK singles chart for 29 weeks during the period of May 1963 to April 1964. On top of that, the label released ten Number One albums by The Beatles during the decade, plus a host of other best-selling albums.

However, during the mid '60s, Martin became disenchanted with EMI, who were reluctant to pay him a royalty on the million-selling records which he produced for them, and along with fellow producers Ron Richards and John Burgess he left to form AIR Studios. Parlophone was then put into the hands of Norman Smith, the man who actually engineered The Beatles' test session in 1962. Later he was to record hit records for EMI under the name Hurricane Smith, and he would also oversee the launch of the progressive label Harvest.

While The Beatles, The Hollies, Cilla Black and Scaffold continued to fly the flag for Parlophone, there were few new additions to the roster until the early '70s, when all of the Beatles released successful solo projects bearing the Parlophone album prefix P and singles prefix R, despite the fact that they carried the group's own Apple logo design. By 1976, the only active artist on Parlophone was Paul McCartney's Wings, whose massive two-million-selling hit 'Mull Of Kintyre' was actually released on the Capitol label (EMI's company in America), although it bore the number R6018.

By the '80s, the use of the Parlophone logo was no longer a pre-requisite for being signed to and issued on the Parlophone label. Both Dexy's Midnight Runners and Duran Duran had hit records released by Parlophone that had R prefixes but no £-sign logos. Thomas Dolby and The Pet Shop Boys were successfully added to the label's roster at this time, along with Morrissey, who – despite being a Parlophone artist – insisted that his records actually came out on the traditional HMV label.

As the '90s neared, so Parlophone's list of hit singles and albums began to mount up again, with the duo of Marc Almond and Gene Pitney, Kim Appleby and EMF emerging as new names on the label. Queen also switched to Parlophone, moving over from EMI.

No 1
Singles -
Albums -

No 1
Singles **41**
Albums **35**

PARLOPHONE

Still firmly entrenched as a part of EMI, Parlophone has continued focus on developing new British talent. An association with the influential label Food brought Blur, Jesus Jones and Dubstar to the label, along with the likes of Radiohead, Supergrass, Mansun and Kylie Minogue. Colplay added to the success of the famous £-sign label, which also poignantly appeared at the top of the charts on George Harrison's final album, released in 2002 after his death.

Peerless MCM

PEERLESS

ALTHOUGH THE COMPANY MADE ITS FIRST
RECORDINGS IN MEXICO IN 1933, it did not officially
operate under the name Peerless until 1947. In the 50-plus
years since then, the company has become established as
one of Mexico's leading record companies.

Specialising in northern Grupero and Sonora music,
Peerless's roster includes artists such as Margarita and Los
Acosta, alongside early catalogue recordings of Cuban dance
bands and Mambo music. In 2001, Peerless was acquired by
Warner Music International's Mexican affiliate to operate
alongside the MCM company which was bought in 1996.

The Sound of
Philadelphia

Philadelphia
International
Records

No 1
Singles **3**
Albums -

No 1
Singles **1**
Albums -

PHILADELPHIA INTERNATIONAL

KENNY GAMBLE AND LEON HUFF, FOUNDERS OF PHILADELPHIA INTERNATIONAL RECORDS IN 1971, have publicly acknowledged that their role models were Berry Gordy and Motown. 'Motown, a black-owned label that had a tremendous amount of activity, was an example to us,' commented Gamble. 'Before we started PIR we went to Detroit and had interviews with Norman Whitfield and Eddie Holland.'

Gamble and Huff first met in the early '60s, formed Excel Records together in 1966 (which soon became Gamble Records) and began writing and producing hits for artists such as Jerry Butler, Dusty Springfield, Laura Nyro and Wilson Pickett. In 1969 they formed Neptune Records, which featured emerging acts from Philadelphia such as The O'Jays, The Three Degrees and Billy Paul.

A marketing and distribution deal with Columbia encouraged Gamble and Huff to form Philadelphia International in 1971, and the roster was increased to feature Harold Melvin And The Blue Notes, Thelma Houston and MFSB. Selling millions of records across the board, Philly International branched out to form the subsidiary label TSOP (The Sound Of Philadelphia) in 1974, which released Dee Dee Sharpe, The Intruders and Archie Bell. Their deal with CBS finally expired in 1982. Gamble and Huff, who had been accused of receiving payola in the mid '70s, decided to reduce the size of their company before returning to the fore with the likes of Phyllis Hyman and Shirley Jones through EMI.

Philadelphia International's catalogue is still owned by Gamble and Huff, and remains a constant best seller on EMI. Meanwhile, the label entered the hip-hop arena at the end of the '90s with the label Uncensored Music, featuring the company's first new signings for a decade, Damon and No Question. Uncensored also maintains links with the company's founders by having at its head the founders' sons Caliph Gamble and Leon Huff II.

No 1
Singles **4**
Albums **2**

No 1
Singles **34**
Albums **3**

PHILIPS

THE DUTCH ELECTRONICS GIANT PHILIPS FOUNDED THEIR MUSIC DIVISION UNDER THE NAME PHILIPS PHONOGRAPHISCHE INDUSTRIES IN 1950, and prospered in the early years from their own signings and from a European licensing deal with CBS. In fact, the Philips label held the UK Number One spot for 22 weeks between August and December 1956 thanks to the American label's star acts Doris Day, Frankie Laine and Johnny Ray, and also their own UK star Anne Shelton. In America, after the acquisition of Mercury in 1960, Philips successfully launched Paul And Paula and The Four Seasons, and released the only Belgian and French records ever to reach the top spot in the US charts by The Singing Nun and Paul Mauriat respectively.

However, Philips and the German company Siemens established a joint venture company in 1962 which linked Philips' PPI and Siemens' Deutsche Grammophon music operations. The new company was renamed Phonogram and included the Philips labels among its imprints, along with its roster of artists such as Dusty Springfield, The Four Pennies and The Walker Brothers. The emergence of the Vertigo and Mercury labels, within the Polygram operation formed in 1972 by the merger of Phonogram and Siemens' pop label Polydor, left Philips as an outlet for MOR material for nearly a decade.

However, in the early '80s, a new Philips Classics label was established alongside the Decca and Deutsche Grammophon divisions, and Philips was re-established as a major classical operation, thanks to artists such as the tenor Andrea Bocelli and the violinist Andre Rieu. The label forms part of the Universal classics and jazz division, and has been merged with the company's historic Decca Records label.

No 1
Singles **2**
Albums -

No 1
Singles -
Albums -

PHILLES

PHIL SPECTOR, ROCK MUSIC'S ENFANT TERRIBLE OF RECORD PRODUCTION, first met up with experienced producer and publisher Lester Sill in the late '50s, when Spector asked to work with Sill and his partner, Lee Hazlewood, the men responsible for Duane Eddy's hits. While Spector moved on to work with legendary writers Leiber and Stoller and began to write and produce his first hit records, Sill went on to launch the small Gregmark label, but in 1961 the pair finally became formal partners in the Philles label, the title being a combination of their names: Phil and Les.

The Crystals brought the first hits to Philles, but Spector and Sill managed only a year together before Spector bought out his partner in 1962 to become America's youngest label chief, at just 21 years of age. Darlene Love, singer with both The Crystals and Bob B Soxx And The Blue Jeans, was joined on the roster by The Ronettes before Spector signed white duo The Righteous Brothers from the Moonglow label. Their 1965 worldwide hit 'You've Lost That Lovin' Feelin'' brought Spector and his famed wall of sound to world prominence. However, the American failure of another massive production number – Ike and Tina Turner's 'River Deep, Mountain High' – in the following year signalled the end of Spector's label.

After releasing one album from Lenny Bruce, Philles was closed down in 1967 by Spector, who didn't return to production work for two years. Spector's famous Philles recordings have been re-released over the years, and his catalogue now rests with the Universal Music Group.

No 1
Singles **1**
Albums -

No 1
Singles -
Albums -

PLANTATION

JEANNIE C RILEY'S ONE AND ONLY POP HIT BROUGHT
PLANTATION RECORDS THEIR ONLY MAJOR SUCCESS,
when 'Harper Valley PTA' topped the US singles chart in 1968.
Label founder Shelby Singleton worked out of Louisiana, with
Mercury stars such as The Big Bopper and Johnny Preston,
before moving to subsidiary label Smash with Brook Benton
and Bruce Channel, ultimately launching his own Plantation
Records. Singleton's success with Riley led him to pull off his
biggest coup, when he bought Sun Records from founder Sam
Phillips in 1969 and re-issued the original Sun recordings
through his SSS and Sun International Corporation.

No 1
Singles **3**
Albums **1**

No 1
Singles **33**
Albums **25**

POLYDOR

THE LABEL THAT TODAY BOASTS MILLION-SELLING POP ACT BOYZONE
AT THE HEAD OF ITS POP ROSTER WAS FIRST FORMED WAY BACK IN 1924,
when the Siemens-owned German company Deutsche Grammophon company launched
a second arm of their company under the name Polydor.

After '50s chart success with French singer Caterina Valente, Polydor had to wait
for over a decade before Jimi Hendrix took the name back into the UK charts in 1967.
In the same year, Hendrix and The Who switched to the in-house label Track, while
Robert Stigwood entered into production deals with Polydor and launched (with limited
success) the labels Creation and Reaction.

German orchestra leader James Last was a consistent success for Polydor,
charting with over 60 albums between 1967 and 1995, while the '70s heralded a
golden age of pop for the label. Slade, New Seekers, The Rubettes and Rory Gallagher
were major players in the label's fortunes, while Stigwood's RSO Records became
an important world-wide force. American acts The Osmonds and James Brown were
both released in the UK by the Polydor operation, while in the US the label became
home to chart-toppers Gloria Gaynor and Vangelis. With the formation of Polygram,
Polydor operated alongside sister labels Mercury, Fontana and Vertigo but succeeded
in retaining its profile thanks to The Jam, Sham 69, Barclay James Harvest and
Scottish comedian Billy Connolly.

During the past two decades, Polydor has succeeded with Level 42, Roxy Music,
Ian Brown, Cast and, more recently, S Club 7. Part of Universal Music since 1999,
Polydor launched Boyzone's Ronan Keating on his successful solo career, alongside
chart toppers Girls Aloud and Daniel Bedingfield.

PONY CANYON INC.

PONY CANYON

OWNED BY THE GIANT JAPANESE MEDIA COMPANY NIPPON BROADCASTING SYSTEMS, Pony Canyon was set up in 1966 initially to exploit the growing market for cassette sales in petrol stations. However, it expanded to emerge as a successful record company, linking with the UK label Echo in 1993 and breaking major-selling Japanese acts such as Ayumi Shigemori, Kentarou Hayami, Tohko And Himawari Kids, The Dango Choir and recent 3 million-selling act Glay. Pony Canyon remains one of Japan's – and the world's – top five independent music companies.

No 1
Singles -
Albums -

No 1
Singles 7
Albums -

POSITIVA

EMI RECORDS IN THE UK LAUNCHED its successful dance imprint Positiva in 1993 under the guiding hand of Nick Halkes.

Hits from Barbara Tucker, The Vengaboys, Spiller, Frogma, Alice Deejay and Room 5 led to Positiva being regularly voted the UK's best dance label.

The label, which has links in the US with Strictly Rhythm, launched sister imprint Additive in 1996 and continues to operate within EMI.

POSTCARD

LAUNCHED IN SCOTLAND IN 1980 AND CLOSED
THE FOLLOWING YEAR, POSTCARD RECORDS came
into being on the back of Britain's 1970s punk explosion and
delivered two successful Scottish bands.

Founder Alan Horne signed both Orange Juice, featuring
Edwyn Collins, and Aztec Camera to Postcard, but the departure
of both acts to major labels led to the company's demise in
1981, after releasing just a dozen singles and one album.

In 1992, Horne reactivated the label and released an
Orange Juice compilation album, alongside new releases from
Paul Quinn and Nectarine No 9.

No 1
Singles -
Albums **2**

No 1
Singles -
Albums -

PRIORITY

BRYAN TURNER STARTED THE PRIORITY LABEL IN 1985 AS AN OUTLET FOR RAP COMPILATION ALBUMS. Ten years later, after adding the likes of Ice Cube and Ice-T to the label's roster, he sold half of the company to EMI for $55 million. In 1993, Ice-T's disputed album Home Invasion was released by the label, and in addition to newer acts such as Mack 10 and Tru this forged a link with Death Row Records, and led to a profitable distribution deal with No Limit.

Priority's continued dominance of American rap and hip-hop music attracted EMI again in 1997, when they acquired the remaining 50% of the company for a further reported $63 million. The company remains one of the overlords of rap music thanks to deals with influential labels such as Rap-A-Lot, P2K and Bee Mo Easy.

No 1
Singles **3**
Albums -

No 1
Singles **2**
Albums -

PRIVATE STOCK

AFTER EXECUTIVE LARRY UTTAL WAS OUSTED
FROM BELL RECORDS IN 1974, he set up his own
Private Stock label as essentially a label for pop singles. Within
a year the label enjoyed its first US Number One, with Frankie
Valli, and this was followed by the success of pianist Walter
Murphy in 1976. However, Private Stock's biggest hits were
to come a year later with David Soul, the star of a TV cop
show *Starsky And Hutch*, who returned to a long-forgotten
singing career to top the charts on both sides of the Atlantic
before the end of the decade.

Private Stock's last chart records came in 1978, courtesy
of Soul and Australian singer Samantha Sang, and the label
closed down in the same year. Most of the artists retained the
rights to their recordings for Private Stock, which was part
owned by EMI in the UK. Uttal, who later opened up a movie
business in London and a travel company in New York, died
in 1993 at the age of 71.

PROFILE

NEW YORK RAP LABEL PROFILE ACTUALLY BEGAN
LIFE IN THE LATE '70S AS A DIVISION OF MCA RECORDS
UNDER THE NAME PANORAMA. One-time MCA employee
Cory Robbins and writer and producer Steve Plotniki (who
worked with Panorama act Front Page) bought the label from
MCA, renamed it Profile and issued dance records by the likes
of Grace Kennedy and Lonnie Love.

In 1981, the duo Dr Jeckyll And Mr Hyde (featuring Love)
brought a much-needed hit record and financial security to
Profile with 'Genius Rap'. Two years later, up-and-coming rap
stars Run-DMC signed to Profile and ensured the label's
reputation as a major rap company.

Profile also signed Rob Base and Dana Dane alongside Run-
DMC, but in 1994 Robbins sold his half of the company to
Plotniki, who re-named it Profile Entertainment. In 1999, Arista
completed the acquisition of Profile in a deal which allowed
founder Plotniki to run his own dance and progressive labels.

No 1
Singles -
Albums -

No 1
Singles **9**
Albums **6**

PWL

THE UK'S MOST SUCCESSFUL PRODUCTION TEAM
OF THE '80s, PETER WATERMAN, MATT AITKEN AND
MIKE STOCK, were also involved in PWL Records, which
was launched in 1987 and became the UK home of Australian
soap stars Kylie Minogue and Jason Donovan. Stock, Aitken
and Waterman (SAW) produced major hits for Dead Or Alive,
Hazell Dean, Mel And Kim, Bananarama and Rick Astley before
Waterman set up PWL, which went on to achieve sales of over
100 million records from 120 international hits.

The UK's top singles label in both 1989 and 1990, when
it enjoyed eleven Top 40 hits from just 16 releases, PWL's
focus was almost entirely on Minogue and Donovan. However,
both left the label in the '90s, just before the SAW team also
split up.

Waterman continued to run PWL Records, with its
subsidiaries PWL Continental and PWL America, but only Dutch
group 2 Unlimited maintained the label's high chart profile.
After a brief joint venture with the Warner Music International
company, PWL was bought out by WMI in 1997, and very soon
afterwards the name PWL Records disappeared, to be replaced
by Coalition Records, which in turn was phased out in 2000.

PYE

PYE WAS ALREADY AN ESTABLISHED HOUSEHOLD NAME IN THE UK,
thanks to its sales of radios and televisions, before it entered the record business
in 1953 with the acquisition of Nixa, a small independent label that focused on
continental recordings. The Polygon label – which was formed in 1949 and on which
were launched the careers of child star Petula Clark and singer/disc jockey Jimmy
Young – was added in 1955, and this led to the official launch of Pye Records,
although the imprint Pye Nixa was retained for a further four years.

In 1957, Lonnie Donegan was the first Pye Nixa artist to have a UK Number One
record, and he was later joined at the top of the charts by Marion Ryan, Chris Barber
and Emile Ford And The Checkmates, whose 1959 hit 'What Do You Want To Make
Those Eyes At Me For?' was Pye Nixa's last chart-topper before the label became
known simply as Pye.

The company created Pye International in 1958 as an outlet for recordings
licensed from small US labels, and for 21 years it was the imprint for hits from such
influential American companies as Chess, Wand, A&M, Kama Sutra, Buddah and
King. Artists who had UK releases on Pye International include Ritchie Valens, Etta
James, Chuck Berry, Bo Diddley, The Kingsmen, Lovin' Spoonful, The Lemon Pipers
and Ohio Express.

Tony Hatch, the man who later wrote the theme tunes for TV soaps *Crossroads*,
Emmerdale Farm and *Neighbours*, was at the forefront of Pye's success in the '60s
and '70s as A&R man, writer and producer. He worked with established acts like
Donegan and Clark, as well as new signings The Searchers, Sandie Shaw and Jackie
Trent, who was later to become Mrs Hatch.

Pye's fortunes were further enhanced by the signing of The Kinks, The
Foundations, Kenny Ball, and two of the UK's most successful MOR acts, Val Doonican
and Max Bygraves, whose *Singalonga...* series of albums were massive sellers in
the '70s. The company had also previously launched two subsidiary labels, Pye
Golden Guinea (with Joe Brown) and Piccadilly, but these were replaced in the '70s
with the Dawn label, home to Mungo Jerry. Meanwhile, Brotherhood Of Man brought

No 1
Singles -
Albums -

No 1
Singles **32**
Albums **4**

PYE

Pye a Number One in 1976 with their Eurovision Song Contest winner 'Save All Your Kisses For Me'.

The '80s saw Pye's fortunes begin to decline as the company's rights to the name Pye expired because of a deal that had been struck over 20 years earlier. In 1959, the Associated Television (ATV) company had bought 50% of the record company from Pye, who sold the remaining half to ATV in 1966. However, the rights to the name Pye lasted only until 1980, at which point the record label was renamed Precision Records And Tapes (PRT). After ATV was acquired by Australian businessman Robert Holmes A'Court's Bell Group, the music side of the company floundered because of lack of interest.

With its healthy back catalogue of important UK recordings, along with some influential jazz titles, PRT was sold on by Bell to Roy Richards in 1987, who re-introduced the Nixa label as a classical imprint. Two years later, PRT changed hands again when it was purchased by Castle Communications, a UK company which specialised in catalogue exploitation. In turn, Castle, together with the Pye catalogue, was acquired by Sanctuary in 2000.

PACIFIC – see Liberty

PAGE ONE – see DJM

PALM PICTURES – see Rykodisc

PANORAMA – see Profile

PAPILLON – see Chrysalis Group

PATHÉ – see Columbia/EMI Music

PEAK – see Concord

PENALTY – see Tommy Boy

PICCADILLY – see Pye

PLAYBOY JAZZ – see Concord

POINT BLANK – see Virgin

POLYGON – see Pye

PRIVATE MUSIC – see BMG Entertainment

PROLIFICA – see EMI

No 1
Singles **1**
Albums -

No 1
Singles -
Albums -

Q

QWEST

LEGENDARY MUSICIAN, A&R MAN, COMPOSER AND PRODUCER AND COMPOSER QUINCY JONES became the owner of a record company in 1982, when he formed Qwest Records in Los Angeles. Jones had previously been a jazz player with Dizzy Gillespie and Lionel Hampton, head of A&R at Mercury for seven years between 1961 and 1968, writer of music for movies and TV shows including *Ironside* and *I-Spy*, and producer of hits for Lesley Gore, Aretha Franklin and Michael Jackson.

The Qwest label continued the Jones success story by notching up a US Number One hit single from Patti Austin and James Ingram in 1983. Jones, the man behind the legendary USA For Africa charity single 'We Are The World' in 1985, maintained a high profile throughout the '80s and '90s. He continued to release his own musical offerings on Qwest, a joint venture with the Warner Music Group, of whom Jones was ultimately named a senior vice-president.

QUEEN – see King

No 1
Singles -
Albums -

No 1
Singles **6**
Albums **1**

R

RAK

AFTER STARTING HIS MUSICAL CAREER AS ONE OF THE MOST
BROTHERS, Mickie Most graduated to become one of the world's leading record
producers and pop entrepreneurs before he hit new levels of pop success with his
own label, RAK Records.

Most's production success began in the '60s with groups such as The Animals
and Herman's Hermits, along with solo stars Lulu, Jeff Beck and Donovan, who all
appeared on a range of different labels. In 1969, he formed RAK Records, employing
Nicky Chinn and Mike Chapman as the label's in-house writers and producers, who
worked alongside his own studio skills. He defined his method of song production
as 'find good songs, go in the studio, make good records and go home'.

For ten years, RAK was home to a host of Britain's biggest pop acts, including
Suzi Quatro, Mud, Hot Chocolate, Smokie and Kim Wilde, and the label enjoyed six
Number One singles in the UK. During that time the label was licensed to EMI, who
finally bought the company and its catalogue from Most in 1979. The man who
founded the label expressed no regrets about the deal: 'You can't live in the past and
keep looking back. After I sold RAK, I just moved on.'

Although EMI bought the RAK company and recordings from Most, they weren't
allowed to use the RAK name or logo on subsequent releases, and the '90s re-release
of Hot Chocolate's recordings appeared on the EMI label. Most, who chose the name
RAK, after the American system of selling discs from racks, and used his yacht (which
sank) as an illustration of the label, died in July 2003.

RCA

THE FAMOUS RCA COMPANY ENTERED THE RECORD BUSINESS IN 1929, and was home to Elvis Presley, the worlds' most successful rock 'n' roll singer, for over 20 years. In that first year, RCA (the Record Corporation of America) bought the original Victor Talking Machine, which had been established in 1901 by Emile Berliner, the inventor of the gramophone.

The company Victor already owned the rights in America to the world-renowned dog-and-trumpet logo, having acquired them from the British Gramophone Company's HMV division. Its most important early recordings were classical works by the likes of Stokowski, Toscanini and Caruso, many of which appeared on the prestigious Red Seal label, and these records established the Victor label as America's leading record label.

David Sarnoff, who was chairman of RCA in its early days, wrote of the impact of the innovation of recorded music and his company's Victrola phonograph in those far-off days: 'The little terrier listening to His Master's Voice now hears it with entire fidelity, and Caruso sings anew from the revolving stage made possible by new plastic discs created by advances in the science of chemistry.' When RCA was determined as the name for the company's record label, Victor – which had also been responsible for some of America's earliest jazz recordings – became a sub-sidiary label, alongside its sister Bluebird imprint.

In the '30s, RCA was at the forefront of swing music, with Fats Waller, Benny Goodman, Glen Miller and Tommy Dorsey leading the most popular big bands of the day, and record sales – which had dropped dramatically at the beginning of the decade – began to boom again. In 1940, The Tommy Dorsey Orchestra featuring Frank Sinatra notched up the label's first Number One record in the newly-created *Billboard* chart of best-selling retail records with 'I'll Never Smile Again'.

Just before the start of World War Two, RCA launched 'Project X', a secret study into the record and phonograph situation. This resulted in the first public demonstration of the RCA-Victor 45rpm system in 1949, which featured the first complementary record and changer, the first distortion-free record and the first

RCA

single-sized records, all of which were fashioned from a new, unbreakable brand of lightweight plastic. While the 45rpm single revolutionised the pop music business, RCA successfully introduced new artists such as Perry Como, Dinah Shore and Eddie Fisher alongside classical idol Mario Lanza, and were among the first labels to make a commitment to the production of stereo recordings, which was introduced in the '50s.

However, despite these stars and a new recording system, RCA ceased to be the power they had been in the record industry until a man called Colonel Tom Parker arrived with a singer from Tupelo, Tennessee. Elvis Presley signed to RCA in 1955, after a few years with Sun Records, and over the next two decades he transformed the company's fortunes and the face of popular music. His first releases in the UK (because RCA was licensed through EMI) actually appeared on the HMV label, bearing the same dog-and-trumpet logo as his American RCA releases.

The success of soundtrack albums culminated in RCA's release of the music of South Pacific, which topped the UK's first-ever LP chart, published in weekly music paper *Melody Maker* in November 1958. However, the extraordinary success of Presley dominated the label's release schedule throughout the late '50s and '60s, although Sam Cooke and Neil Sedaka were among the handful of other RCA acts who also made an impact.

The '70s saw country singers Jim Reeves, Dolly Parton and John Denver begin to emerge, alongside rock group Jefferson Airplane, Lou Reed, Harry Nilsson and Hall And Oates. A generation of British artists was also signed to the RCA label in the UK, including The Sweet, David Bowie and Bucks Fizz, and in the '80s The Eurythmics, Rick Astley and Fairground Attraction were also added to the roster.

In 1985, when RCA found itself slipping down the world record table, the company attempted to buy the Ariola/Arista music division of the German Bertelsmann company, but instead General Electric stepped in and bought RCA. Uninterested in the record business, General Electric soon sold RCA to Bertelsmann, who set about creating the Bertelsmann Music Group (BMG). Curiously, General Electric

No 1
Singles **50**
Albums **32**

No 1
Singles **77**
Albums **38**

RCA

retained the ownership of the dog-and-trumpet logo, which they license to BMG/RCA for use on their recordings.

The success of Mr Mister, SWV and Bruce Hornsby took RCA into the '90s as part of BMG alongside new stars such as The Dave Matthews Band, The Verve Pipe and Christina Aguilera. At the same time, UK signings Natalie Imbruglia, M-People, Take That, Gary Barlow and Annie Lennox also maintained a high chart presence for the label first made famous by Tommy Dorsey and Elvis Presley.

Under the direction of Clive Davis, and linked with his company, J Records, after 2002, RCA's newest hit acts included American Idol winner Kelly Clarkson, Christina Aguilera and The Foo Fighters. In the UK, Westlife, 5ive and Pop Idol arrivals Will Young and Gareth Gates helped to earn RCA an impressive 16 UK Number One singles in just three years. Among these, Young and Gates's version of 'Suspicious Minds'/'The Long And Winding Road' became the UK's historic 938th Number One in 2002, 50 years to the day after the start of the British singles chart.

No 1
Singles **2**
Albums -

No 1
Singles -
Albums -

RED BIRD

DESPITE HAVING A LIFE SPAN OF ONLY AROUND
TWO YEARS, Red Bird Records – the brainchild of hit
songwriters Jerry Leiber and Mike Stoller – made a
considerable impression on the US record charts. Having
previously launched and closed Spark Records, Leiber and
Stoller followed up with Red Bird in 1964 and enlisted the help
of established songwriting teams such as Barry and Greenwich,
Goffin and King and Mann and Weil. All-girl groups The Dixie
Cups and The Shangri-Las were at the forefront of Red Bird's
impressive track record of over 20 Top 100 US singles in just
two years, but Leiber and Stoller closed Red Bird in 1966, as
they were more interested in writing and producing than running
a record label.

REGAL ZONOPHONE

No 1
Singles -
Albums -

No 1
Singles 2
Albums -

REGAL ZONOPHONE

EMI'S TWO FRONT-LINE LABELS, Columbia and HMV, had operated budget labels back in the '30s under the names Regal and Zonophone respectively. In that decade they were combined to create the Regal Zonophone imprint, which offered recordings by the Salvation Army and also handled some Okeh, Victor and Columbia releases from America. Music hall and variety acts such as Gracie Fields and George Formby steered the label towards the '60s, and the Salvation Army group The Joy Strings provided the label with its début chart entry in 1964.

Successful '60s pop producers Denny Cordell and Tony Visconti – both of whom had successful independent production companies – later signed with Regal Zonophone, delivering the likes of The Move and Procol Harum (both from Deram), which were followed by Joe Cocker and T Rex. In the '70s, as these production deals ended and the acts moved to new labels, so Regal Zonophone lost its impetus and EMI ceased to use it as a major pop label. However, the Regal imprint was re-introduced at the end of the '90s.

No 1
Singles -
Albums -

No 1
Singles **3**
Albums -

RELENTLESS

UK URBAN LABEL RELENTLESS EMERGED IN 1999
as a joint venture between label founders Shabs Jonaputra
and Paul Franklyn and the influential Ministry of Sound
organisation.

Home to hit acts such Artful Dodger, the controversial So
Solid Crew, Pied Piper and Daniel Bedingfield, Relentless went
into voluntary liquidation in 2003 despite selling over 2 million
singles in just over three years. Founders Jonaputra and
Franklyn, having won the rights to the name Relentless, formed
a new joint venture with Virgin Records, operating from Virgin's
London offices.

No 1
Singles **9**
Albums **9**

No 1
Singles **3**
Albums **2**

REPRISE

REPRISE RECORDS STANDS OUT AS ONE OF THE MOST ENDURING AND FAMOUS LABELS EVER FOUNDED BY A RECORDING ARTIST. Frank Sinatra formed Reprise in 1960, when he reached the end of his contract with Capitol Records, and installed himself at the head of the label. While his own records were among the first Reprise releases, Sinatra added close friends Sammy Davis and Dean Martin to the label, along with his daughter Nancy, before completing a deal with Warner Bros Films in 1963. Under this agreement, Sinatra made movies for the studio and they in turn bought Reprise from him.

Under the direction of the Warner Bros Records operation – which had as an executive the legendary Mo Ostin, who had run Reprise for Sinatra – hits came from the likes of Trini Lopez and Freddy Cannon. A deal with the UK label Pye brought Petula Clark and The Kinks to Reprise in America, as well as Jimi Hendrix, while Frank and Nancy Sinatra hit the Number One spot both together and as solo artists.

Reprise also sought new American talent, and added Gordon Lightfoot, Neil Young, Joni Mitchell, The Beach Boys (via their own Brother Records label) and Chicago to the roster, and maintained the label's position as a home to contemporary American music throughout the '70s and '80s. The Kinney Corporation's acquisition of Warner Bros Records resulted in Reprise ultimately becoming part of the Warner Music Group, together with its parent label. Today it features Eric Clapton (via his own Duck imprint), Green Day, Filter, Disturbed, multi-million-seller Josh Groban (via 143 Records) and Grammy winners Steely Dan, following Giant's merging into Reprise.

No 1
Singles 1
Albums -

No 1
Singles -
Albums -

RHINO

ESTABLISHED TODAY AS THE WORLD'S FINEST
CATALOGUE LABEL, Rhino grew out of a store called Rhino
Records, which was opened in Los Angeles in 1973 by Richard
Foos and store manager Harold Bronson. The pair ventured
into the record business in 1978 with Wild Man Fischer's first
release before concentrating their efforts on a joint passion
for pop music, much of which was no longer available to buy.
The label's state-of-the-art mastering and quality repackaging
was first seen in re-issues of Ritchie Valens, The Monkees and
The Turtles.

The label achieved a Number One single in the US in 1987
with the re-release of Billy Vera's 'At This Moment', originally
released in 1981. Rhino have also acquired the labels Roulette
and Sugar Hill, and bought catalogue material by major artists
such as Aretha Franklin, Ray Charles, and The Righteous
Brothers. With interests in film, television and video packages,
Rhino is now a wholly-owned division of the Warner Music
Group, which completed its acquisition of Rhino in 1999.

No 1
Singles **1**
Albums **1**

No 1
Singles **2**
Albums **2**

RIVA

THE MAN BEHIND RIVA RECORDS WAS ROD STEWART'S MANAGER, BILLY GAFF. The label was set up in 1975 as a vehicle for Stewart, who appeared on Riva in the UK while remaining on the Warner Bros label in America. The only other major signing to Riva was John Cougar Mellencamp, who recorded for his manager's label between 1977 and 1986. Both Stewart and Cougar moved to new management and record companies, however, and the Riva label was eventually wound up.

No 1
Singles -
Albums **1**

No 1
Singles -
Albums **2**

ROADRUNNER

FOUNDED IN THE NETHERLANDS IN 1981, Roadrunner Records established itself as one of the largest independent labels in America until Universal Music's Island Def Jam group acquired a 50% stake in 2001.

Founder Cees Wessels focused on European rock acts in the label's early years and acquired rival Dutch company Arcade Music Group, with its successful MOR and pop compilation operations, in 1999. While the Arcade name was adopted for Roadrunner's European activities outside the Netherlands, Roadrunner continued to prosper in the US and, with the success of acts such as Slipknot, Nickelback, Type O Negative and Coal Chamber, over 50% of the company's sales came from America.

Wessels' sale of half of his company to Island Def Jam for a reported $33 million ended Roadrunner's distribution deal with Edel and saw Universal take over distribution, while Roadrunner retained responsibility for all marketing, sales and promotion.

ROCK

SINCE 1979, WHEN SAM AND JOHNNY DUANN FOUNDED ROCK RECORDS, the Taiwanese operation has become established as south-east Asia's largest and most successful independent record company.

Publishers of the magazine Rock, the Duann brothers, acted as licensees for international majors in Taiwan before expanding and setting up their own offices, signing local artists throughout the region. The artist Sarah Chen brought the label its first multi-platinum album in 1989, and she was followed by artists such as Jutoupi, Richie Ren and Karen Mok. Rock's focus on Mandarin repertoire, as well as its own operations in 13 countries throughout the Asian Pacific region, make it a major force in the huge Chinese record market market, but Taiwan's economic uncertainty and music piracy problem have reduced Rock's performance despite local best sellers Mayday and Tapestry.

No 1
Singles **4**
Albums -

No 1
Singles **3**
Albums **2**

ROCKET

IN THE MID '70s, ELTON JOHN signed to his own Rocket Records after having left DJM Records in 1976 and immediately struck gold with his first-ever Number One record, his duet with Kiki Dee 'Don't Go Breaking My Heart'. John had actually started the label a year earlier, and after Neil Sedaka took the Rocket imprint to the top of the charts in America in 1975, John himself switched to Rocket from MCA in America in 1976. The label also offered a new opportunity in America for Cliff Richard, who charted on Rocket with two late-'70s releases.

The label also offered solo releases from Kiki Dee, as well as Colin Blunstone and Blue, and Elton John's 1978 hit 'Song For Guy' was a tribute to a Rocket messenger who had been killed in a car crash. The label eventually became home to just John, via Polygram Music's Mercury division, and in 1997 Rocket took its place in pop history as the label on which the world's largest-selling pop single was released, John's tribute to Princess Diana, 'Candle In The Wind 1997'.

Two years later, and now as part of the Universal Music Group which had acquired Polygram, Rocket was closed down by the controlling Island Def Jam division, and John switched to Island.

US

No 1
Singles **3**
Albums **8**

UK

No 1
Singles -
Albums **5**

ROLLING STONES

THE ROLLING STONES LAUNCHED THEIR OWN LABEL, with its famous tongue logo, in 1971 with the Number One album *Sticky Fingers*. The label has been used almost exclusively for the group's own product, although reggae star Peter Tosh briefly appeared as a Rolling Stones artist in the late '70s.

Having signed to Decca in 1964, The Stones stayed on Decca and London (in America) until they signed to Atlantic in 1970 and formed Rolling Stones Records within Atlantic's Atco subsidiary. The group retained the logo design (along with the slightly dubious COC and CUN prefixes) throughout their Atlantic days and on their move to EMI outside the US.

The group signed to CBS in 1986, where their only chart album appeared with a CBS identity. While their last releases have appeared on Virgin Records, following a worldwide move to that label, the famous Rolling Stones logo is still prominent.

No 1
Singles -
Albums -

No 1
Singles -
Albums **1**

ROUGH TRADE

GEOFF TRAVIS STARTED UP HIS ROUGH TRADE BUSINESS as a West London record shop in 1976, specialising in imports and indie releases. A growing distribution business led him to expand and form the Rough Trade record label in 1978. Launched with Metal Urbain as its first act, Rough Trade later branched out into reggae and avant-garde pop before punk band Stiff Little Fingers brought the label its first major hits. Operating as a co-operative, Rough Trade branched out to set up tour management, publicity and publishing services for its signed artists, which included Robert Wyatt, Aztec Camera, The Fall and Scritti Politti.

American acts including Jonathan Richman and Pere Ubu arrived at Rough Trade looking for their music to be released in the UK, but the label's biggest success came with the arrival of The Smiths, who dominated Rough Trade's schedule for four years from 1984. Flushed with the success that they brought, Travis moved on and launched the Blanco Y Negro label in partnership with Warner Music UK, while Rough Trade looked to The Sundays to carry on The Smiths' good work after they left the label.

However, with fewer and fewer hits and a collapsing distribution operation, Rough Trade's fortunes began to fade, and in the late '90s the Rough Trade label, name and recordings were sold off in a variety of different deals which included Zomba acquiring Rough Trade Germany and One Little Indian buying the name and back catalogue rights. In 2002, under the guiding hand of original founder Travis, who had re-acquired the name, a new Rough Trade emerged as a joint venture with Sanctuary Records and delivered new signings The Libertines and, for the UK, hit US indie band The Strokes.

No 1
Singles **6**
Albums -

No 1
Singles -
Albums -

ROULETTE

ESTABLISHED MUSIC PUBLISHERS MORRIS LEVY
AND PHIL KHALS FORMED ROULETTE RECORDS
IN NEW YORK IN 1956, but within a year it was sold to
producers Hugo Peretti and Luigi Creatore, who produced
the label's Number One hit by Jimmie Rodgers and later
went on to found Avco Records. The two producers sold
Roulette back to Levy a couple of years later, and new labels
such as Gone and End were integrated into Roulette. The
label found chart success in the early '60s with Joey Dee
and The Essex before Tommy James And The Shondells, the
label's final chart-toppers, arrived in 1969.

Roulette then focused on repackaging its catalogue
material and on signing a limited number of acts, as well as
acquiring American independent operations such TK
Records. Before his death in the mid '90s, Levy sold the
Roulette catalogue to EMI and to Rhino (for America only).

No 1
Singles **17**
Albums **5**

No 1
Singles **5**
Albums **4**

RSO

AUSTRALIAN ROBERT STIGWOOD worked for The Beatles' manager Brian Epstein in his NEMS organisation before branching out on his own into films and music and introducing million-selling group The Bee Gees to the world. The producer of Broadway musical *Jesus Christ, Superstar*, Stigwood developed the idea for the film *Saturday Night Fever*, which features a soundtrack by The Bee Gees, whom he managed and originally signed to Polydor in 1967.

Stigwood had formed the Creation and Reaction imprints in the same year, in partnership with Polydor, but despite the success of supergroup Cream the two labels faded away. He created RSO – again in association with Polydor, but distributed by Atlantic in America – in the early '70s with a roster which featured Eric Clapton, The Bee Gees, Yvonne Elliman and Frankie Valli, alongside RSO's soundtrack successes *Saturday Night Fever* and *Grease*, both of which sold in excess of 30 million copies. The latter became the biggest-ever movie musical.

Stigwood's RSO label first topped the US charts in 1974, and then set a new record for US Number One hits when, between December 1977 and May 1978, the label held the top spot for 21 consecutive weeks thanks to six separate singles by The Bee Gees, Andy Gibb, Player and Elliman. By 1981, Stigwood ended his day-to-day involvement with RSO Records, while The Bee Gees and Clapton both moved to new labels. The label currently remains part of Polydor, who retain the rights to the RSO catalogue.

RECORDS

No 1
Singles **2**
Albums **5**

No 1
Singles -
Albums -

RUFFHOUSE

THE LABEL THAT BROUGHT KRISS KROSS AND LAURYN HILL to the attention of the world was founded by two men who insisted on basing their Ruffhouse company in Conshohocken, in their home state of Pennsylvania. Local musician Chris Schwartz and producer Joe Nicolo (who worked with Jazzy Jeff And The Fresh Prince) began the first Ruffhouse venture in the mid '80s before linking with Columbia Records in a joint venture in 1989. Schwartz has gone on record as saying that his Ruffhouse label is not an easy label with which to land a deal. 'In the hip-hop community, Ruffhouse is perceived as the hardest label to get to signed to because we're very low-key, but if people do get a deal they know that we will do at least two albums. We only have seven or eight things on the roster.'

Early acts Blackmail and Mack Money were followed by the label's first hit artists, Kriss Kross and Cypress Hill, who brought major success to Ruffhouse. The arrival of The Fugees finally established the label, and solo projects from the group's members Pras, Wyclef Jean and ultimately Lauryn Hill took Ruffhouse to a new level. However, in 1999 Schwartz and Nicolo decided to call it a day and dissolved both their partnership and the Ruffhouse label. The label's existing roster of acts remain on the Ruffhouse/Columbia imprint, but no new signings have been added to the label.

Schwartz re-emerged with RuffNation Records, a new joint-venture label with Warner Bros Records, while Nicolo formed his own label, Judgement Records, whose roster included Kriss Kross.

No 1
Singles **1**
Albums **3**

No 1
Singles -
Albums -

RUTHLESS

CREDITED WITH BEING THE LABEL WHICH FOUNDED GANSTA RAP, Ruthless was established in mid-'80s Los Angeles by Eazy-E (Eric Wright), who was to form his own label's star turn NWA (Niggas With Attitude), comprising Dre, Ice Cube and DJ Yella. Following the success of NWA, Eazy-E added Above The Law, Bone Thugs N Harmony and JJ Fad to the roster as Ruthless continued its rise to the top of the gansta rap genre. He shocked friends and enemies alike in 1991 by donating $2,500 to the Republican Party and attending a fund-raising event for George Bush Sr's presidential campaign.

From its founding through to the early '90s, Ruthless collected a host of platinum and multi-platinum records for multi-million sales. The label continued to flourish up until 1995, when Eazy was diagnosed as having contracted the AIDS virus. He died in the same year, at the age of 31. His widow continued to run his label within the Relativity organisation, which had distributed Ruthless recordings since 1993.

RYKODISC

IN 1983, WITH THE EMERGENCE OF A NEW FORMAT CALLED THE COMPACT DISC, Rob Simmonds and Don Rose met up and decided to form Rykodisc as a CD-only label. Taking the name from the Japanese for 'sound from a flash of light', Rykodisc also adopted the distinctive marketing tool of packaging all of its releases in green jewel boxes. With new partners Arthur Mann and Doug Lexa, Rykodisc was launched with an album from Jim Pepper, established its credentials with the 1986 release of eight Frank Zappa titles, and achieved its first major success in 1991 with Grammy award winner Mickey Hart.

The business of marketing existing catalogue brought David Bowie, Elvis Costello and Yoko Ono to Rykodisc, while the company also acquired new labels, including Hannibal, Gramavision and Tradition. Ex-Hüsker Dü frontman Bob Mould went on to head the roster, alongside Bruce Cockburn, Morphine and Kate And Anna McGarrigle. Ryko's international business is based around the UK operation formed in 1987, which oversees distribution outside the UK and US.

In 1999, having left Island Records at Universal Music, Chris Blackwell acquired Rykodisc for a reported $35 million as part of his new Palm Pictures venture. Ryko de-merged from Palm Pictures in 2001 and added the American indie Restless Records alongside a roster of artists including Joe Jackson, Robert Cray and Kelly Joe Phelps.

RADAR – see Demon/Stiff

RADIOACTIVE – see MCA

RARE EARTH – see Motown

RAWKUS – see Mushroom

REACTION – see Polydor/RSO

REALWORLD – see Virgin

RED ROBIN – see Enjoy

RED SEAL – see BMG Entertainment/RCA

REPUBLIC – see Universal

REV-OLA – see Creation

RIDE – see Ministry Of Sound

RISING TIDE – see Universal

RUFF RYDERS – see Def Jam

RECORDS

S

BMG A&R EXECUTIVE and *Pop Idol* judge Simon Cowell formed his joint venture company with BMG in 2000 but didn't officially name it S Records until 2002.

His role as a pioneer of the *Pop Idol* TV talent show format, in conjunction with 19 Management's Simon Fuller, gave him access to contestants in the original UK show and its US counterpart, *American Idol*.

Pop Idol artists Will Young and Gareth Gates (managed by 19 Management) and American winner Kelly Clarkson head the S artists roster, alongside Irish boy band Westlife, with releases going out under the BMG banner.

In 2003, BMG acquired Cowell's stake in S Records in a reported £20 million-plus deal which linked Cowell to the label for five years.

SANCTUARY

FORMER CAMBRIDGE UNIVERSITY STUDENTS ROD SMALLWOOD AND ANDY TAYLOR formed the original Sanctuary company in 1976 as an artist management business, with Iron Maiden as their first discovery.

Adding the likes of Poison, Wasp and The Human League to the management roster, Sanctuary expanded into merchandising and a booking agency before launching Sanctuary Records in the early 1990s as part of the Sanctuary Group, which also covers TV production and book publishing.

The 45,000-track catalogue of Castle Music, including Immediate, Pye and Translatlantic, was added in 2000, followed by leading reggae label Trojan, with its catalogue featuring Bob Marley, Dennis Brown and Jimmy Cliff, and US label CMC with Blue Öyster Cult and Lynyrd Skynyrd.

A joint venture with Rough Trade Records was formed in 2002, including The Strokes for the UK, while Sanctuary's metal label, Metal Is, boasted Bruce Dickinson, WASP and Motörhead. American reggae label RAS Records was added in 2003.

Sanctuary Records' roster of direct signed artists now boasts Alison Moyet, KISS, Dolly Parton, The Kinks, Stevie Winwood, Morrissey (whose recordings will be issued on the former Trojan imprint Attack), and The Pet Shop Boys in America.

SAVOY

SAVOY RECORDS WAS FOUNDED IN NEWARK, New Jersey, in 1942 by Herman Lubinsky, and was named after the famous ballroom in New York's Harlem district. Savoy issued early recordings by the likes of Coleman Hawkins and Billy Daniels, and is regarded as being one of the first real R&B labels of note.

The '50s saw Esther Phillips (then known as Little Esther), Little Sylvia (who later co-founded Sugar Hill Records as Sylvia Robinson), Johnny Otis and Big Maybelle all record for Savoy, but the emergence of rock 'n' roll put R&B labels under great pressure and, as a result, Lubinsky turned Savoy into a gospel label. He died in 1974, and it was alleged that the label was bought by Clive Davis, then boss of Arista. The label's original R&B recordings have since become much-sought-after items.

No 1
Singles **4**
Albums **1**

No 1
Singles **2**
Albums -

SBK

AMERICANS STEPHEN SWID, MARTIN BANDIER AND CHARLES KOPPELMAN formed the production company SBK in 1989 following their purchase of the CBS music publishing division in 1986. The trio then sold the publishing operation to EMI Music Publishing for a reported $295 million, and Bandier and Koppelman then formed the SBK record label. The label enjoyed an impressive run of hits in its initial years with Vanilla Ice, Wilson Phillips, Technotronic and the million-selling phenomenon Teenage Mutant Ninja Turtles. The label is still owned by EMI, but Koppelman is no longer a part of the company and Bandier now runs EMI Music's publishing arm. SBK is no longer a frontline imprint.

No 1
Singles **3**
Albums -

No 1
Singles -
Albums -

SCEPTER/WAND

FLORENCE GREENBERG, WHO HAD EARLIER BEEN INVOLVED WITH HER OWN LABEL TIARA RECORDS, launched the Scepter label in 1959 with an all-girl quartet called The Shirelles, who were then the only act signed to the new label. On the back of the group's successful single 'Dedicated To The One I Love', Greenberg launched the Wand subsidiary label two years later, with Tommy Hunt and Chuck Jackson as featured artists. The Shirelles carried on to produce hits for Scepter until they left the label in 1967. After that it was left to The Isley Brothers, BJ Thomas and Dionne Warwick (who reached the US Top Ten with eight Scepter releases) to maintain the label's position at the forefront of American soul and R&B. No longer an active company, Scepter/Wand releases are now only available through specialist re-issue companies.

SILVA SCREEN

UNDER THE GUIDANCE OF REYNOLD DA SILVA, SILVA SCREEN RECORDS was launched in London in 1986 and focused on film soundtrack and classical music releases.

Among the label's soundtrack albums are Il Postino and The Pink Panther, plus compilations of film and television music, while Lesley Garret and The Crouch End Festival Chorus are among the Silva Classics releases.

Over 400 albums are available from the Silva Records group of labels, which includes the Hip Bop jazz imprint, with releases from Lenny White and Michal Urbaniak, and the German CMP Records, acquired in 1997, featuring Jack Bruce, Mick Karn and John McLaughlin.

SIRE

	No 1	**No 1**
	Singles **12**	Singles **7**
	Albums **4**	Albums **4**

SIRE

VETERAN RECORD EXECUTIVE SEYMOUR STEIN, who began his career with Billboard before moving on to King Records and Red Bird Records, formed the Sire label in New York in 1966 in partnership with producer Richard Gotteher. While the name came from mixing the first two letters of Seymour with those of Richard, Stein says that it was also chosen as a tribute to Syd Nathan and King Records.

Stein established early links with the UK blues label Blue Horizon and hit the US charts with albums from The Climax Blues Band and Focus before taking Sire into the Warner Bros Records family in 1976. The label emerged with a list of leading new wave exponents including The Ramones, Talking Heads and Richard Hell and attracted UK acts such as The Rezillos, The Pretenders and '60s beat group The Searchers.

With Stein still running the label as part of Warner Bros, Sire continued to add more major acts from both North America and the UK. The discovery and signing of Madonna to the label in 1982, where she stayed for a decade before moving over to found her own Maverick imprint, was followed by residencies by Depeche Mode, The Smiths, kd lang, Erasure, Seal and Barenaked Ladies. The signing of rap star Ice T in 1987 brought a new emphasis to Sire, although controversy over his rap lyrics caused him to move labels in 1992.

After a brief spell as head of Elektra Records, Stein returned to Sire in 1998 to resurrect the label as a free-standing entity within the Warner Music Group and set about placing those acts who had remained with Warner Bros. Morcheeba, Everything, Mandy Barnett and The Tragically Hip were among those that were added before Sire linked with London Records in 2000 to form Sire London. Three years later, Sire Records was re-established as a stand-alone label within Warner Bros Records and under Stein's continuing leadership the label has a new roster of acts including The Distillers and the Vox Blondes.

No 1
Singles -
Albums -

No 1
Singles 1
Albums -

some bizzare

SOME BIZARRE

STEVO, THE ECCENTRIC MANAGER OF MARC ALMOND, was the force behind Some Bizarre Records, which he formed in the early '80s. The label made its first impression with the compilation album *The Some Bizarre Album*, which was linked with Soft Cell in Stevo's initial deal with Phonogram. Boasting the likes of Soft Cell, The The, Cabaret Voltaire and Classix Nouveau on its roster, throughout its history Some Bizarre experienced periods of great influence, coupled with financial uncertainty and stories of the trashing of record company offices and deals involving sweets as part of an advance.

The label continued to be home to interesting new talent while Marc Almond – whose duets with the likes of Gene Pitney and PJ Proby were released by other labels – remains its best-known and best-selling artist, even though his last hit for the label was in 1995.

Sony Music

SONY MUSIC

SONY MUSIC CAME INTO BEING IN 1988 when the giant Sony Corporation acquired the highly successful CBS Records Group for $2 billion and put one of America's most famous companies into Japanese ownership.

The company's origins can be traced back to the original Columbia label, which was formed in 1887, and was expanded with the addition of the Okeh label in 1926. The American Record Company (ARC) bought the Columbia label in 1934, but four years later the Columbia Broadcasting System (CBS) took control and, in the '50s, added the Epic label alongside the established CBS label. The Epic division of Sony includes 550 Music and Okeh while Columbia consists of Aware, Ruffhouse and Relativity.

In 1968, an initial link with Sony was established via a joint venture in Asia, but when Sony completed their acquisition 20 years later the CBS name and logo were retained by the original Columbia Broadcasting System corporation. This led to the introduction of the Columbia label alongside Epic in America, and, after the company struck a deal with EMI in the late '80s to buy out their rights to Columbia internationally, the development of these two labels moved to the forefront of Sony Music's world-wide operation. In the UK, the company's network of distributed independent labels – including Loaded/Skint and Independiente – operate alongside two wholly-owned subsidiaries: S2 and Oasis's own Big Brother imprint.

No 1
Singles -
Albums **1**

No 1
Singles -
Albums **1**

SONY CLASSICAL

THE CURRENT SONY CLASSICAL OPERATION – which boasts the soundtrack to the film *Titanic*, the world's biggest-selling classical album – was formally established in 1927 by the American Columbia company, under the Masterworks banner.

In 1948, Columbia Masterworks had the honour of issuing the first 12" recording, following Columbia's introduction of the new format in the same year. Featuring Nathan Milstein with the Philharmonic Symphony Orchestra of New York playing Mendelssohn's violin concerto in E minor, the 33^1/$_3$rpm long-playing record sold for $4.85. During the next three decades, Columbia Masterworks' roster featured Isaac Stern, Pablo Casals and Vladimir Horowitz, alongside Eugene Ormandy and Leonard Bernstein. They also issued original cast recordings of successful musicals such as *South Pacific* and *My Fair Lady*.

In 1980, the company was renamed CBS Masterworks in line with the promotion of the CBS name, but following Sony's acquisition of the CBS Music operation the classical operation was renamed Sony Classical in 1990. In addition to setting up the subsidiary Vivarte label, Sony Classical continued to bolster its roster with the likes of Kathleen Battle, Zubin Mehta, Wynton Marsalis, Yo-Yo Ma, Bobby McFerrin and award-winning conductor/composer John Williams.

Continuing the company's long history of releasing best-selling cast and soundtrack recordings, James Horner's original work for the film *Titanic* resulted in massive worldwide sales of over 27 million for the chart-topping album of 1998, which was issued on Sony Classical's sister label Epic and featured Céline Dion's hit 'My Heart Will Go On'.

Sony Classical also hit the headlines with child singer Charlotte Church, whose début album *Voice Of An Angel* made the 13-year-old Welsh singer the youngest artist ever to have a UK Number One classical album and a Top Five entry in the UK album charts. Her success was followed by Michael Bolton's album of classical arias and Pope John Paul's Abba Pater release, plus a host of film soundtracks.

SPV

FOLLOWING ITS LAUNCH IN HANOVER IN 1984, GERMAN METAL/ROCK LABEL SPV acted as distributor for Roadrunner Records before branching out to sign emerging metal acts, such as Sodom and Destruction. Other artists followed and today's SPV roster features the likes of Saxon, Steve Hackett and German Dance-award winners Delerium.

Established as one of Germany's top-five independent record companies, Hanover-based SPV has links as German distributor to labels such as Sanctuary, Inside Out, Snapper and Naidoo while its own releases are issued in America through Navarre. In 2000, SPV founder Manfred Schutz sold a 51% stake in his label to media company In-Motion.

No 1
Singles -
Albums -

No 1
Singles **1**
Albums **4**

S2

A WHOLLY-OWNED DIVISION OF SONY MUSIC UK, S2 took its name from the company's former offices in London's Soho Square. Boasting a roster featuring million-selling dance act Jamiroquai, soul singer Des'ree and the rock band Reef, S2 is presided over by veteran A&R man Muff Winwood, a former member of '60s band The Spencer Davis Group and brother of Stevie Winwood.

SPECIALTY

ART RUPE CHANGED THE NAME OF HIS ORIGINAL 1946 LABEL JUKE BOX RECORDS TO SPECIALTY IN ORDER TO SHOW THAT HIS LABEL SPECIALISED IN A PARTICULAR STYLE OF MUSIC: blues and gospel. Early signings included Roy Milton, Guitar Slim, Percy Mayfield and The Soul Stirrers, featuring a young Sam Cooke. The LA-based label gradually developed into one of the world's leading R&B and rock 'n' roll outlets, featuring Lloyd Price ('Lawdy Miss Clawdy') and the incomparable Little Richard, whose Speciality hits included 'Tutti Frutti', 'Lucille' and 'Good Golly, Miss Molly'.

In Joe Smith's Off The Record, Little Richard recalled his early days with Specialty: 'When I went to Speciality, [Art Rupe] didn't like my songs. He wanted me to sing like BB King, but I didn't feel it. It was all too slow.' The loss of Richard and Cooke in the late '50s and the emergence of new pop music had a negative impact on Specialty's fortunes, and Rupe wound down his label in the '60s. Reissues were regularly made available, however, and in 1991 Fantasy acquired the label.

No 1
Singles -
Albums -

No 1
Singles 2
Albums -

STATESIDE

AFTER EMI LOST THE RIGHTS TO DISTRIBUTE AMERICAN REPERTOIRE FROM CBS AND RCA IN THE LATE '50S, the company needed an outlet for big-selling American hits which they wanted to acquire for release in the UK. Their solution was the formation of Stateside, a label created to be the home of a variety of American artists and records signed to smaller, emerging US labels which didn't have a UK contract. The Supremes' first UK chart-topper, 1964's 'Baby Love', was Stateside's first big hit, while the likes of ABC's Tommy Roe, United Artists' Gene Pitney and Vee Jay's The Four Seasons were among the most successful Stateside acts.

When EMI began to set up formal long-term licensed label deals with American labels such as Motown, MCA and Asylum in the early '70s, the company no longer required Stateside and the imprint was retired to the EMI archives.

No 1
Singles **3**
Albums **1**

No 1
Singles -
Albums **1**

STAX

AFTER THEIR ORIGINAL VENTURE, SATELLITE RECORDS, had been foiled because of a rival company's prior claim on the name, Jim Stewart and his sister Estelle Axton launched the hugely influential Stax Records label in 1961.

Based in a run-down theatre in Memphis, Tennessee, Stax got its name from the first two letters of the surnames Stewart and Axton. Stewart, a local bank clerk and country fiddle player, was a white guy who invested in black talent – such as Rufus Thomas and his daughter Carla – in order to get Stax up and running. Linking with the influential Atlantic label for distribution gave Stax genuine strength in the marketplace, and they delivered a roster of hugely successful and influential soul acts such as Booker T And The MG's, William Bell, Isaac Hayes, Eddie Floyd, Sam And Dave and The Staple Singers.

Memphis was at the heart of American soul music in the '60s, and acts jumped at the chance to join the Stax label. Isaac Hayes, who appeared on its Enterprise subsidiary, recalls: 'Jim Stewart heard me play and asked if I wanted a job. Booker T had gone off and Stax needed a keyboard player and a staff musician. I said OK.'

Stax's subsidiary label, Volt, was the company that was to deliver to Stewart and Axton their greatest success. Otis Redding, who first arrived at Stax as a valet (parking attendant) for an auditioning act and pleaded to be given a chance to sing, made Stax/Volt household names. However, shortly after his death in 1967, and with the arrival of Wilson Pickett to the label, Stax ended its fruitful association with Atlantic, who retained ownership of all of the Stax masters.

Stax was reborn as part of the Gulf And Western empire in 1968 and enjoyed success with Johnnie Taylor, Judy Bell and William Bell before Stewart – whose sister had left the company with the termination of the Atlantic deal – successfully bought back his label in 1970, thanks to a loan from Polydor Records. However, Stewart left Stax within a year, leaving his partner Al Bell to complete a distribution deal with Columbia.

In 1973, the company ran into trouble. Plagued by accusations of financial irregularities and with its major artists leaving the label, Stax was finally declared bankrupt in 1976. Its assets were bought at auction by Fantasy Records, who continue to repackage and re-release the Stax catalogue.

No 1
Singles -
Albums -

No 1
Singles **2**
Albums **1**

STIFF

THE LEGENDARY BRITISH INDEPENDENT LABEL STIFF RECORDS came into being in 1976 when band managers and pioneers of '70s pub rock Dave Robinson and Jake Riviera decided to launch their own label, with the benefit of a £400 loan from the late Lee Brilleaux, singer with Dr Feelgood. The label's first release – carrying the catalogue number BUY 1 – was Nick Lowe's 1976 single 'So It Goes'. Stiff supported their artists with innovative marketing ideas such as the 'Bunch Of Stiffs' tour, which featured Lowe, Dave Edmunds, Elvis Costello and Wreckless Eric, and issuing the notorious T-shirt bearing the slogan 'If It Ain't Stiff It Ain't Worth A F***'.

After the early days of selling Stiff releases by mail order and from the back of a van, the label entered into a distribution agreement first with Island and then with CBS. With Ian Dury and Elvis Costello among its first major album sellers, Stiff was established as one of the UK's leading independents and a model for a host of new labels. In 1977, Riviera's departure to Radar Records (along with Costello and Lowe) left Robinson to add new talent, including Lena Lovich, Jona Lewie, Graham Parker and Madness. By the end of 1980, Stiff's annual turnover was in excess of £3.5 million, and in its first six years of trading the label released 150 singles bearing the BUY prefix and saw 30% of them reach the UK chart.

The introduction of reggae, soul and oddball UK acts such as Tenpole Tudor continued to keep the Stiff name alive, along with some help from hits by Dave Stewart and The Belle Stars and releases by Rachel Sweet, Devo and The Plasmatics, who were licensed from American new wave labels.

In 1984, Stiff was incorporated into Island Records at the same time that Madness left the label and The Pogues arrived. The deal wasn't a success, though, and in 1986, Robinson – who had become head of the Island/Stiff operation – recaptured control of a newly independent Stiff Records. However, the label's new life was short lived as a serious cashflow crisis brought Stiff to verge of collapse, when ZTT Records – owned by Jill Sinclair and her producer husband Trevor Horn – stepped in and bought the label's assets for a reported £300,000. The name of one of the music industry's truly pioneering labels still remains part of ZTT.

SUB POP

MUSIC MAGAZINE EDITOR BRUCE PAVITT and promoter Jonathan Poreman established Sub Pop in 1986 and alerted the world to Seattle's greatest musical contribution: grunge. The signing of acts such as Green River (who spawned Pearl Jam), Tad, Soundgarden and, naturally, Nirvana – who released their début album for the label in 1989 – focused huge attention on Sub Pop and its artists. Even after Nirvana left the label in 1991, Sub Pop continued to attract acts, and even after a minority share was sold to the Warner Music Group it remained a haven for rock and authentic grunge acts. However, following Pavitt's departure from the label and a downturn in its fortunes, Sub Pop widened its horizons and added acts such as Shins, The Vue and Beechwood Sparks to the roster.

RECORDS

SUE

THE ORIGINAL SUE RECORDS LABEL WAS
ESTABLISHED in New York by Henry Jones in 1957, and
because of its location (near the famous Apollo Theater) it
attracted aspiring R&B acts.

The label's first success came with Bobby Hendricks and
Don Covay, and then, in 1960, Ike and Tina Turner arrived
at the label and produced seven US chart hits before they
left in 1962. After releasing Sue product in the UK through
Decca, the label switched to a licensing agreement with
Island, which eventually resulted in a split in the ownership
of the name. In the UK, the label was used as a vehicle for
soul and blues acts such as James Brown and BB King before
it disappeared in the late '60s. Jones (also known as Juggy
Murray) retained ownership of the label in the America but
failed to repeat his success of the early '60s. In 1968, he
sold the Sue masters to United Artists but retained the name
and has re-activated it over the years, with limited success.

SUGAR

HUNGARIAN-BORN LADISLAO SUGAR STARTED HIS FIRST MUSIC PUBLISHING BUSINESS, Melodi, in Milan in 1932 and expanded into the larger Suvini Zerboni company in 1935.

After taking over full ownership in 1948, Sugar joined forces with rival company CGD (General Records Company) in 1952 and ran the new company throughout the 1960s when leading Italian acts Adriano Celentano and Johnny Dorelli headed the roster.

A partnership in Italy with CBS led to the creation of CBS Sugar in 1970, which was run by Sugar's daughter-in-law and former CGD artist, Caterina Caselli. In 1977 the Sugar CBS deal ended, followed by founder Ladislao Sugar's death in 1981, aged 85. In 1989 the family sold CGD to Warner Music International, but retained much of the company's important catalogue.

A new Sugar record label was formed with Caselli's son Filippo Sugar at the helm and the discovery in 1993 of Andrea Bocelli re-established Sugar as a major music company with interests in Italian retail stores and radio stations.

SUGAR HILL

THE FIRST LABEL TO BE TOTALLY DEVOTED TO RAP MUSIC was launched in New York in 1974 by Sylvia Robinson (the former Little Sylvia) and her husband Joe. They named the label after a street in the city's Harlem district, and it should not be confused with the bluegrass and roots label of the same name that was founded in North Carolina in 1978. With Sylvia's track record of singing and producing (she had worked with Ike and Tina Turner and Shirley And Co), the Robinsons went on to start such labels as Vibration and All Platinum, which boosted the careers of Chuck Jackson and Candi Staton.

When All Platinum ran into trouble, the husband-and-wife team set up Sugar Hill Records, after receiving financial assistance from Roulette Records' boss Morris Levy, who provided them with space in his Broadway offices. The label's first record – recorded in one take for a reputed $700 – was 'Rapper's Delight' by The Sugar Hill Gang. The ground-breaking, 15-minute-long 12" record wasn't an immediate hit with Joe Robinson, who has gone on record as saying: 'No 15-minute record ever got played on radio. But all it had to do was get play anywhere, and it broke.' The record sold a reported two million copies in America and went a long way to delivering rap music to the world.

After The Sugar Hill Gang, the label added Sequence, Grandmaster Flash and Melle Mel to the roster, and in the early '80s Robinson bought out Levy and moved to New Jersey. The label then began to experience financial difficulties, and artists began to leave Sugar Hill. To make things worse, a proposed deal with distributors MCA fell through, although the major did purchase the Robinsons' Chess masters. By 1986, Sugar Hill was insolvent and forced into bankruptcy. In 1995, re-issue specialists Rhino Records acquired the Sugar Hill catalogue and all of their unreleased masters.

GOLDEN TREASURE SERIES

SUN

THE MEMPHIS-BASED LABEL SUN RECORDS, which discovered, signed and sold Elvis Presley, was founded in 1952 by a former DJ from Alabama named Sam Phillips, who died in Memphis in 2003, aged 80.

Phillips began operating in Memphis in 1950 with his company the Memphis Recording Service, which made personal records and recorded weddings and bar mitzvahs. He was also keen to work with local black talent, and soon found himself recording the likes of Bobby Bland, Howlin' Wolf, BB King, Big Walter Horton and Jackie Brenston (whose 1951 hit 'Rocket 88' has been described as the first ever rock 'n' roll record) for Chicago and Los Angeles labels such as Chess, Checker, Modern and RPM.

Phillips soon established Sun Records, which ran alongside his recording service on Memphis' Union Avenue, and Rufus Thomas's 1953 record 'Bear Cat' (a play on the more famous 'Hound Dog') brought the label its first hit. Other artists on Sun's early roster included Junior Parker, Little Milton and a group of former Tennessee State Penitentiary inmates called The Prisoners, who released 'Just Walkin' In The Rain' three years before Johnny Ray's hit version.

In August 1953, Elvis Presley took advantage of Phillips' recording service to make a personal record as a gift for his mother. Marion Keisker, a local radio personality, was in the studio and when she asked Presley who he sounded like, he replied, 'I don't sound like nobody.' When he returned in January 1954 to make a second personal record, Presley caught Phillips' attention, and within six months he was signed to the label, releasing his début single 'All Right Mama' in July 1954.

Presley made only four more singles for Sun, with 'Baby Let's Play House' becoming the first Elvis record on the Sun label to appear on the national charts. He moved to RCA Records in 1956 when Phillips sold Presley's contract, singles and unreleased masters to the major for $35,000, with Presley receiving a further $5,000. RCA had managed to beat off Atlantic's bid to sign the boy from Tupelo.

With Presley gone, Phillips began to assemble a new roster of Sun stars, quickly bringing Jerry Lee Lewis, Carl Perkins, Johnny Cash, Charlie Rich and Roy

SUN

Orbison to the label. Orbison, whose major hits also came after he left Sun, commented on his time with the Memphis label to Joe Smith in *Off The Record*: 'Sun Records had mystique. I headed off there because Presley did and Carl Perkins did. Sun was near enough and I was young enough, and it was all super-exciting.'

Sun became home to rock 'n' roll classics such as 'Blue Suede Shoes', 'I Walk The Line', 'Great Balls Of Fire', 'Good Golly, Miss Molly' and 'Ooby Dooby', but one by one Perkins, Cash, Rich, Orbison and finally (in 1963) Lewis followed Presley out of Sun Records. While the label struggled to compete with the rapidly-growing major record companies and the cost of national distribution, Sun nevertheless continued to record new artists during the '60s. However, the likes of Bill Justis, Mickey Gilley, Sonny Burgess and The Jesters – who featured Phillips' sons Knox and Jerry – couldn't repeat the success of Sun's golden years.

In 1969, Phillips – who had become a major shareholder in the emerging Holiday Inn hotel company – sold Sun Records to the music publisher and producer Shelby Singleton, who added a handful of acts and marketed the original Sun recordings through his own SSS label in America and through Charly Records in the UK.

In 1990, one of the most sought-after Sun sessions was finally released on record when a record by The Million Dollar Quartet was issued. The session dated back to December 1956, when Elvis Presley (by then an RCA star) returned to the Sun studio on the day that Carl Perkins was recording 'Matchbox', with Jerry Lee Lewis on piano. Although Johnny Cash was also in town, and was photographed with the trio for a publicity shot, the session that was recorded later that day actually featured just Presley, Perkins and Lewis, who jammed their way through gospel, pop and rock tunes. So The Million Dollar Quartet was just a threesome after all.

Swan

No 1
Singles 1
Albums -

No 1
Singles -
Albums -

SWAN

THE PHILADELPHIA LABEL SWAN sprang to prominence in 1964 when it delivered The Beatles' second American Number One hit, 'She Loves You'.

After EMI's American company Capitol turned down The Beatles' first singles, their manager Brian Epstein took to licensing them to small American labels. He leased 'She Loves You' to Swan in 1963, but it only became a hit after Capitol finally broke The Beatles with 'I Want To Hold Your Hand' and Swan were able to successfully re-activate it in January 1964.

In the '50s, America's longest-serving DJ and TV host Dick Clark was an investor in Swan and other small record companies, but after a congressional investigation following up allegations of payola involving record companies and radio stations he gave up his label interests.

No 1
Singles -
Albums **4**

No 1
Singles -
Albums **4**

SWAN SONG

AFTER ISSUING THEIR FIRST FIVE ALBUMS ON ATLANTIC, rock band Led Zeppelin and their heavyweight manager Peter Grant launched Swan Song in 1975 as a vehicle for their own releases. The label was funded in the main by the huge earnings received by the band from their series of record-breaking American tours from the early '70s. Over a seven-year period, until 1982, five Led Zeppelin albums appeared on Swan Song, which continued to be distributed by Atlantic. The band also added their own signings to the label, which included Bad Company, Maggie Bell and The Pretty Things, while the band members Jimmy Page and Robert Plant both released solo albums on Swan Song.

Led Zeppelin split up in 1982, after the death of drummer John Bonham, and this also signalled the beginning of the end for Swan Song, as the acts began to drift away to other labels. Grant, the band's guru and the overlord of their empire, died in 1995.

SATELLITE – see Stax

SERIOUS – see Mercury

SINGER – see Gallo

SHELTER – see A&M

SITUATION TWO – see Beggars Banquet Group

SLASH – see London

SMASH – see Mercury/Plantation

SO SO DEF – see Arista

SOURCE – see Virgin

SPARK – see Red Bird

SPITFIRE – see Eagle Rock

STAR-DAY KING – see King

STRETCH – see Concord

STRUMMER – see Universal

SURPRISE – see Island

TELDEC

TELDEC

ESTABLISHED TODAY AS ONE OF THE LEADING CLASSICAL LABELS, Teldec grew out of the ashes of the German company Ultraphon, which crashed in 1932. The hardware and electrical company Telefunken subsequently bought the catalogue and then launched its own recordings under the imprint Telefunkenplatte. After a brief merger with Deutsche Grammophon between 1937 and 1941, Telefunkenplatte linked with Decca in 1948 and the name Teldec was created for the new company.

Teldec was responsible for US repertoire from Warner Bros Records in Germany, and the label chiefs were committed to developing its own roster. To this end, Ernst Mosch, Caterina Valenta and Nikolaus Harnoncourt were signed, and the label also served to handle Decca's releases by The Rolling Stones, Tom Jones and Mantovani in Germany.

Teldec suffered a downturn in business in the '70s and was finally acquired by Warner Music International in 1988, when Ofra Haza and Peter Maffay enjoyed major chart entries. Soon after, the current Teldec Classics imprint was created.

Operating as part of Warner Classics, Teldec boasts a roster which features Nikolaus Harnoncourt, Kurt Masur and Maxim Vengarov. The label was also responsible for the international release of the multi-million-selling 1994 album Three Tenors In Concert, which featured José Carreras, Placido Domingo and Luciano Pavarotti. In 2002, the Germany-based Teldec operation was closed and the imprint, together with a reduced artists-roster, switched to Warner Classics UK.

No 1
Singles -
Albums -

No 1
Singles 2
Albums 3

TELSTAR RECORDS LTD

TELSTAR

MUSIC INDUSTRY EXECUTIVES SEAN O'BRIEN AND NEIL PALMER launched Telstar in 1982 with a government loan of £120,000. The label was formed as a specialist TV compilation marketing operation, and has since grown into one of the UK's leading independent record operations.

Since 1982, Telstar's series of compilation albums has resulted in over 200 chart hits, including two Number Ones in the UK album chart. They have also had more than 20 releases topping the specialist compilation chart, which was introduced in 1989. The label's expansion has also resulted in the undertaking of related activities, such as the founding of the internet company Startle, a distribution operation and advertising production companies.

Teenage stars PJ And Duncan (who later became Ant and Dec) took the Telstar name into the UK singles chart in 1993. With the launch of the Multiply and Wildstar subsidiaries, the company has notched up further chart hits with Connor Reeves, Sash!, Phats And Small and Basement Jaxx, while chart-topper Craig David brought Wildstar and Telstar their first ever UK Number One single ahead of emerging artists Mis-Teeq and Harry. Telstar retains a link with former Creation founder Alan McGee and his Poptones company, including the singles-only label, The Singles Society.

T. K. Records

TK

VETERAN MUSIC MAN HENRY STONE LAUNCHED A NUMBER OF BLUES LABELS DURING THE '50S, such as Chart and Marlin, before emerging with TK as the home to disco stars KC And The Sunshine Band. Stone based himself in Florida, where he operated his labels, distribution centre and recording studio and where Harry Wayne Casey (KC) and Rick Finch also worked. They teamed up to write and produce the first TK Number One, George McCrae's 'Rock Your Baby', before becoming KC And The Sunshine Band and recording hit records for TK between 1975 and 1979. In the UK, all of these hits were issued on the Jayboy imprint.

Anita Ward also hit on the TK-distributed label Juana in 1979 before Stone's label encountered financial difficulties and Roulette Records' Morris Levy acquired the rights to the TK empire.

No 1
Singles -
Albums -

No 1
Singles 1
Albums -

TOMMY BOY

AFTER AN INITIAL CAREER PUBLISHING MAGAZINES DISCO NEWS AND THE INFLUENTIAL DANCE MUSIC REPORT, Tom Silverman borrowed $5,000 from his parents and launched Tommy Boy Records from his New York apartment in 1981. The label's first release (by Cotton Candy) was quickly followed by the hugely successful 'Planet Rock' by Afrika Bambaataa, along with Force MDs and Stetasonic, as Tommy Boy established a reputation as the leading rap and hip-hop label.

Adding new acts such as Coolio, Queen Latifah, De La Soul, House Of Pain and Naughty By Nature, Tommy Boy became an attractive proposition. In 1985, the Warner Music Group stepped in with a successful bid for 50% of the label, although they also allowed Tommy Boy to continue enjoy its indie status by distributing 7" singles through WEA and 12" singles through independent distributors.

Silverman, who was once described by Atlantic founder Ahmet Ertegun as being 'cut from the same cloth as those who started great independent record companies years ago', was instrumental in launching the New Music Seminars in New York in the '80s. In 1990, he linked with MTV to introduce the MTV Party To Go compilation series, and followed this with the Jock Jams collections. He also embarked on a joint venture with Neil Levine in 1995 to create Penalty Records. In 1996, after having previously sold his own 50% share in the company to the Warner Music Group, he bought back 50% of Tommy Boy to re-create the earlier joint venture.

New acts Capone-N-Noreaga (inherited from Penalty when Silverman acquired the outstanding 50% in 1999), Everlast and Prince Paul kept the Tommy Boy name high in the charts, while Silverman – whose motto has been 'I try to find great people and let them do great things' – launched a new division of the label: Tommy Boy Gospel. In 2002, Tommy Boy's catalogue was acquired by Warner Music Group, while Silverman retained rights to the name and a roster of new artists including Amber, Masters At Work and Junior Vasquez. Following his linking with Gut Records in the UK, Silverman opened a German Tommy Boy operation in 2003, based in Berlin and distributed by Edel.

No 1
Singles -
Albums -

No 1
Singles **3**
Albums **1**

TOP RANK

IN THE LATE '50S, TOP RANK WAS RANKED AS ONE OF BRITAIN'S TOP TEN LABELS, alongside the likes of Decca, HMV, Columbia, Pye and Philips. British artists guitar legend Bert Weedon and singer Craig Douglas were among the first Top Rank successes, along with licensed American releases from Freddy Cannon, Sandy Nelson, The Ventures and Dion. The label – which had links with the famous Top Rank film organisation – collapsed in 1960 and was bought by the giant EMI operation.

Actor/singer John Leyton (who was managed by Robert Stigwood) was signed to producer Joe Meek's Triumph label, which leased the 1961 chart-topper 'Johnny Remember Me' to Top Rank. After EMI's acquisition of the label, Leyton remained on Top Rank until he switched to EMI's HMV imprint.

The last major hit on Top Rank came from B Bumble in 1962. The label was then disbanded and laid to rest in the EMI archives.

TOY'S FACTORY

IN A LITTLE UNDER TEN YEARS, Toy's Factory has grown to become a leading label in Japan's emerging independent music sector. Focusing on J-pop and dance releases, Toy's Factory launched the all-girl group Speed (who sold three and a half million copies of their début album), Mr Children, Yazu and My Little Lover, and successfully promoted repertoire from the UK via its licensing deals with the Ninja Tune and Mo Wax labels.

No 1
Singles -
Albums -

No 1
Singles **3**
Albums **1**

TRACK

THE WHO'S MANAGERS, Kit Lambert and Chris Stamp (brother of actor Terence Stamp), linked with Polydor Records to create the Track label, following the success of fellow entrepreneur Robert Stigwood's Reaction label.

Unsurprisingly, the label became home to The Who, who had earlier appeared on both Brunswick and Reaction. However, it was Jimi Hendrix's 'Purple Haze' that became the first Track single in March 1967. Hendrix was signed to Track after Lambert and Stamp had spied him at a London showcase in 1966, although because his first record, 'Hey Joe', was completed before Track was up and running it appeared on the parent Polydor imprint.

Between 1967 and 1973, Track was consistently in the upper reaches of the UK charts thanks to its two superstar acts, along with unlikely pop acts such as Thunderclap Newman and The Crazy World Of Arthur Brown. However, Hendrix's death in 1970 and The Who's move to the major Polydor imprint in 1973 left Track without a future. Today, while the label remains part of Polydor's archives, the Track catalogue is regularly re-promoted.

TRANSATLANTIC

TRANSATLANTIC RECORDS WAS FOUNDED BY AMERICAN NAT JOSEPH after he had spent years trying to find a home for the various American folk outlets which he represented in Britain. Throughout the '60s and '70s, the label provided a home for the finest British folk music. Early releases included readings from a sex manual and recordings by actors Tony Britton and Sheila Hancock. Alexis Korner and the Ian Campbell Folk Group later brought more order to the label, and when Bert Jansch's eponymous début album for Transatlantic was issued in 1966, produced by Joseph, it was reviewed as a landmark album in British folk music.

A host of leading artists made their way to the label, including The Humblebums (whose members Billy Connolly and Gerry Rafferty also recorded as solo performers), Richard Digance, Pentangle, Gordon Giltrap and Ralph McTell. However, pop, rock and disco took their toll on Transatlantic's limited resources, and in 1977 the label was sold. It later re-appeared as Logo Records, featuring Paul Young's Street Band and The Tourists, before Dave Stewart and Annie Lennox moved labels and became The Eurythmics.

Logo closed in 1980, and the label's biggest chart hit had been a re-issued Transatlantic recording of 'The Floral Dance' by The Brighouse And Rastrick Brass Band.

No 1
Singles -
Albums -

No 1
Singles **1**
Albums -

TROJAN

BRITAIN'S LEADING REGGAE LABEL, TROJAN produced nearly 30 hit singles in its brief six-year existence. Island Records founder Chris Blackwell and Pyramid owner Lee Gopthal were the driving force behind Trojan's launch in 1968, together with Jamaican producer Duke Reid, whose nickname of 'the Trojan' gave the label its name. Releasing records by the likes of Jimmy Cliff, Ken Boothe, The Pioneers, Bob And Marcia, Greyhound and Dave And Ansell Collins, Trojan introduced reggae into British mainstream pop music. The label's Big Shot subsidiary went on to release dubious offerings from Judge Dread while Trojan was responsible for the legendary *Tighten Up* compilation series.

After Blackwell left in 1972 to concentrate on the growing Island Records, Trojan continued as part of the B&C empire, until that collapsed in 1975. Ownership of the Trojan catalogue has changed a few times over the years, and recordings were available from a number of outlets until Sanctuary Records acquired the Trojan Records catalogue in 2001 and brought the 10,000 catalogue titles under one roof.

No 1
Singles -
Albums -

No 1
Singles 2
Albums -

2-TONE

JERRY DAMMERS, THE LEADER OF THE COVENTRY-BASED SKA BAND THE SPECIALS, was the driving force behind the 2-Tone label, which he set up in 1979 as the outlet for his band's first releases, including the hit 'Gangsters'. With the label established, Dammers added new acts such as Selecter, Madness and The Beat to 2-Tone, but within a year or two all of them had left the label. The label's final signings, The Bodysnatchers, charted in 1980, but it was left to The Specials to keep 2-Tone in the charts, until the band split in 1985.

Dammers, who named his label to reflect racial integration in his group and its music, was involved in organising the concert celebrating Nelson Mandela's 70th birthday party at Wembley in 1988, and he also performed at the 1990 concert celebrating Mandela's release from prison. Because of his label's earlier link with Chrysalis, the catalogue covering 2-Tone's brief but important six-year history has since been re-promoted.

No 1
Singles **4**
Albums **1**

No 1
Singles **1**
Albums -

20th CENTURY

20TH CENTURY RECORDS OPERATED (not surprisingly) as a division of 20th Century Fox film studios, and notched up its first hits in the '60s with soundtracks from movies such as *Cleopatra* and *Zorba The Greek*.

It was the studios' 1973 movie *The Poseidon Adventure* that brought the 20th Century record label to prominence in the US singles chart, thanks to Maureen McGovern's recording of the film's theme, 'The Morning After'. Soon after, Barry White – who signed for and re-launched the label in 1972 – topped the US charts both with The Love Unlimited Orchestra and also as a solo performer. He was followed by Carl Douglas in 1974, with a recording for the UK Pye company called 'Kung-Fu Fighting', which 20th Century picked up for America.

The label's last major chart success came with two *Star Wars* soundtracks in the late '70s, and when Barry White left in 1979 the 20th Century record label faded from the picture.

TVT

TVT (TELEVISION TOONS) BEGAN LIFE AS A TV THEME MUSIC COMPANY IN 1985 but has grown to become one of America's biggest independents, with a roster which covers the genre of rock, techno and R&B. Under the guidance of owner Steve Gottlieb, TVT's hit bands include Sevendust, Massacre and British band XTC, and the label's turnover in 1999 broke the $40 million mark. Among the world's top 20 independent labels, TVT continues to find success thanks to recordings from Nine Inch Nails, Jimmy Page And The Black Crowes and Lil Jon And The East Side Boys.

TALKIN' LOUD – see Mercury

TAMLA – see Motown

TEAL – see Gallo

10 – see Virgin

THE NEW NO LIMIT – see Universal

13th HOUR – see Mute

THRESHOLD – see Decca

TIARA – see Scepter/Wand

TSOP – see Philadelphia International

TOWER – see Capitol

TRADITION – see Rykodisc

TRIUMPH – see Top Rank

TUG – see Gut

TUSK – see Gallo

No 1
Singles -
Albums -

No 1
Singles 1
Albums -

U

UK RECORDS

JONATHAN KING – POP STAR, record producer, TV host and A&R man – became head of his own record company in 1972, when he launched UK records as a home for his own releases and a wide range of pop creations.

King's career, which started with his own 1965 Top Five hit 'Everyone's Gone To The Moon', expanded into production and A&R (he discovered and first recorded Genesis) before the idea of creating his own label was born. 'I had so many hits as a producer with different labels when I realised that it would make more sense, and be a better deal, to form my own label,' says King, who originally planned to call the company King Of England Records. 'But we got a call from the palace telling us we couldn't use the name, so I chose UK instead. It stood for United King.'

The label's first hit, 'Seaside Shuffle' by Terry Dactyl, was the label's fifth UK release, and was followed by Roy C, Lobo and 10cc, the label's biggest seller, who earned UK its only Number One with 'Rubber Bullets' in 1973. Between these releases, King appeared on UK as himself, and also under the names Shag, Bubblerock, 53rd And 3rd, Sound 9418 and One Hundred Ton And A Feather. By the mid '70s, King, in his own words, was 'bored of it all, meeting with lawyers and accountants meant I couldn't do what I wanted to most, which was to make music.' Before the end of the decade, UK was closed and King was pursuing other interests, while retaining ownership of – and regularly re-issuing – the UK catalogue.

UNITED ARTISTS

FILM STARS CHARLIE CHAPLIN, DOUGLAS FAIRBANKS AND MARY PICKFORD formed the original United Artists company in 1919, together with director/producer DW Griffith, with a view to protecting and representing their interests in the early days of Hollywood movies. The record label emerged out of the burgeoning film studios, and was actively and successfully involved in the film soundtracks business that developed in the '50s. UA was lifted to prominence in the '60s by albums featuring soundtracks from James Bond movies and The Beatles' films *A Hard Day's Night* and *Help!*, along with American stars The Highwaymen – the first US Number One act on the label, in 1961 – and Bobby Goldsboro.

In 1969, United Artists acquired Liberty Records and its subsidiary label, Imperial, but suspended the use of the Liberty label in the early '70s in order to focus their attention on the UA imprint. Their roster boasted pop stars Peter Sarstedt and Shirley Bassey, alongside rock acts Hawkwind, Man and The Groundhogs.

Don McLean's eulogy to rock 'n' roll music, 'American Pie', appeared on UA after the company bought the small Mediarts label, and this song gained worldwide success for the label, along with Paul Anka, Odia Coates, Bill Conti's theme to the movie *Rocky* and Gerry Rafferty's 1978 tribute to London's Baker Street. British pub rock/punk bands Dr Feelgood, The Buzzcocks and The Stranglers went on to add a further dimension to UA's roster, which also boasted ELO through the Jet label.

In 1979, EMI Music purchased United Artists and gradually absorbed the label and its artists into the EMI operations worldwide, in preparation for the return of the United Artists name and label to the original film company.

No 1
Singles **2**
Albums **4**

No 1
Singles **6**
Albums -

UNIVERSAL

AFTER THE FORMER HEAD OF ATLANTIC RECORDS, Doug Morris, took his Rising Tide label to MCA Music in 1995, on the strength of an initial joint-venture agreement, the new MCA subsidiary was renamed Universal Records in 1996. This followed Seagrams' purchase of MCA and the creation of the Universal Music Group, with Morris as chairman. The Universal label's roster boasts the acts Erykah Badu, Billie Myers, The Charlatans and Boyz II Men, and the label enjoys links with Uptown Records, the Cash Money, Republic, The New No Limit and Strummer imprints.

Internationally, the Universal imprint was home to Danish pop group Aqua, who notched up three UK Number One hits for the emerging label, and new US artists such as Nelly and Buster have helped establish Universal as a global record label.

UNIVERSAL MUSIC GROUP

UNIVERSAL MUSIC GROUP

THE UNIVERSAL MUSIC GROUP CAME INTO BEING IN LATE 1996, and after its acquisition of the giant Polygram company at the start of 1999 it is currently established as the world's leading music company.

The long-established American entertainment company, MCA, was bought by the Japanese Matushita corporation in 1990, and was renamed Universal following its subsequent acquisition by the Canadian Seagrams corporation in 1996. MCA, the Music Corporation Of America, was originally founded in 1924 as a booking agency which, after founding a music publishing operation, entered the recording business in 1962 with the purchase of Decca US, including their Coral and Brunswick labels.

After being renamed MCA Records in 1973, the company acquired the Kapp label, and then acquired ABC-Dunhill Records, along with its ABC, Paramount, Impulse, Dot and Dunhill subsidiaries. The purchase of Chess Records in 1985 was followed by the acquisition of Motown Records in 1988 (later sold on to Polygram in 1993), the GRP jazz label and Geffen Records in 1990. Universal Records was set up alongside MCA Records in 1995, and in 1996 Universal acquired a 50% stake in Interscope Records, at the same time launching Hip-O Records

The Polygram music business was created in 1962 following the merger of Phonogram (the music arm of Dutch multinational Philips) with Polydor and Deutsche Grammophon (DG), the music operations of the German company Siemens. The move combined the classical recordings of DG – which was formed in 1898 – with the pop repertoire of Phonogram

UNIVERSAL MUSIC GROUP

and Polydor, and in 1972 they united under the name Polygram. By 1987, Philips had acquired Siemens' share of Polygram, which in turn was launched as a public company in 1989.

Having purchased Decca UK in 1980, including the London Records label, Polygram continued to acquire major labels, adding Island Records to its stable in 1989, A&M Records in 1991 and Motown (ironically bought from MCA) in 1993, along with a majority holding in Def Jam to add to the already established Fontana, Mercury, Vertigo, Verve and Philips imprints.

The world's number one music company, The Universal Music Group, merged the Interscope, A&M and Geffen labels together, linked Island Def Jam with Mercury, and paired the Universal imprint with Motown, while creating a new classics and jazz division combining Decca, DGG, Philips and Verve. In 2000, Universal Music got new owners when the French media/water/transport company Vivendi linked with Seagrams in a £20 billion merger to create Vivendi Universal. Three years later Universal Music and the Univisa Music Group forged a new deal giving Universal distribution rights for Univision's Fonovisa Records, the leading Latin music company.

UNIVISION

FORMED IN 2001 AS A DIVISION OF UNIVISION COMMUNICATIONS, America's leading Spanish-language media company, Univision Music has rapidly expanded to become one of the world's pre-eminent Latin music companies.

Distributed through Universal Music in the US, Mexico and Puerto Rica, Univision's collection of Latin labels include a joint venture with Disa and ownership of regional Mexican label Fonovisa.

Pepe Aguilar and Grupo Mojado lead the Univision roster, while the acquisition of Fonovisa in 2002 for a reported $235 million, added leading Mexican artists such as Los Temerarios and Marco Antonio Solis to the company, alongside Disa's Grupo Bryndis and Los Rehenes.

UNCENSORED – see Philadelphia International

UNI – see MCA

UPTOWN – see MCA/Universal

VAGRANT

INDIE-ROCK LABEL VAGRANT RECORDS emerged in Los Angeles in the early 1990s under the control of founders Rich Egan and Jon Cohen. The label has since entered into an unspecified relationship with Interscope.

Specialising in 'emo-core' artists, Vagrant Records boasts such acts as Reggie And The Full Effect, Alkaline Trio, No Motiv and Dashboard Confessional, whose 2003 US hit album *A Mark, A Mission, A Brand, A Scar* was distributed through indie TVT.

VALE

BARCELONA-BASED INDEPENDENT LABEL VALE MUSIC SPRANG TO PROMINENCE IN SPAIN IN EARLY 2001 on the back of a TV talent show called *Operación Trifuno*.

Artists from the show originally released only albums, which initially led to Vale dominating the Spanish albums chart with up to six titles in the Top Ten in any one week. A change in the rules in 2003 meant that each of the 16 contestants released a single and only those that sold over 20,000 singles went on to make an album for Vale Music.

As a result, Vale have had all Top Ten singles in the Spanish chart on more than one occasion. This has given the company, which was founded in the late 1990s by Eduardo Campoy (one of the founders of an 80s dance label called Max Music), 10 million-plus sales and has established Vale as Spain's leading record company, with a market share of around 25%.

No 1
Singles **1**
Albums -

No 1
Singles -
Albums -

VANGUARD

THE NEW-YORK-BASED LABEL VANGUARD was set up in 1950 by brothers Maynard and Seymour Solomon, and focused on releasing classical recordings until it began to branch out into the field of jazz with the likes of Louis Armstrong and Stéphane Grappelli. However, its first real success came with the folk group The Weavers and 1959 signing Joan Baez, before the considerable blues talents of Buddy Guy, Jimmy Rushing and Otis Rush were also added, amongst others. New folk talent was also recruited in the shape of Buffy Sainte-Marie, Odetta and Tom Paxton, until the label achieved its first (and only) American Number One single in 1963 with 'Walk Right In' by The Rooftop Singers, featuring Erik Darling, who had gone on to replace Pete Seeger in The Weavers five years earlier.

Vanguard's first popular electric rock act, Country Joe And The Fish, were signed in the mid '60s, but the label lay dormant for the much of the '70s before re-emerging for a brief fling with disco in the '80s. The Solomons sold Vanguard in 1986 to the Welk Group, run by the son of legendary American bandleader Lawrence Welk. Both the label's back catalogue and that of its acts, such as Venice, Tab Benoit and Patty Larkin, are currently available.

VARESE SARABANDE

FOR THE PAST 25 YEARS CALIFORNIA-BASED LABEL VARESE SARABANDE has specialised in soundtrack releases, plus catalogue re-issues covering bluegrass to doo-wop and jazz to western swing.

Soundtrack albums from movies such as *The Event*, *The Time Machine*, *Tomb Raider: The Cradle Of Life* and *Terminator 3* line up alongside original cast recordings from *Hello Dolly*, *Best Foot Forward* and *A Grand Night For Singing*. Featured Varese Sarabande artists include Jane Olivor, guitar veterans The Ventures and legendary composer Elmer Bernstein, plus catalogue titles from comedian Flip Wilson, Jimmy Dorsey and Hank Williams.

No 1
Singles **5**
Albums -

No 1
Singles -
Albums -

VEE-JAY

THE HUSBAND-AND-WIFE TEAM OF VIVIAN CARTER AND JIMMY BRACKEN launched Vee-Jay in Chicago in 1953 as an offshoot of their record shop, and named the label after the initials of their first names. The label made its impression with local black acts, Jimmy Reed, John Lee Hooker and The Staples Singers before the subsidiary label Falcon brought them The Impressions and The Dells. The '60s saw influential performers Jerry Butler, Gene Chandler and The Four Seasons establish the name Vee Jay in the American charts.

A deal with British major EMI, based around Frank Ifield's 1962 hit 'I Remember You', gave Vee-Jay access to an unknown British group called The Beatles, whose first releases had been turned down by the UK company's US outlet, Capitol. Vee-Jay issued both 'Please Please Me' and 'From Me To You' without success before Capitol finally broke The Beatles in 1964, and then Vee-Jay released 'Love Me Do' on its Tollie subsidiary and claimed The Beatles' fourth American Number One.

After a short-lived move to Los Angeles, Vee-Jay returned to Chicago in 1965. However, its most successful artists had begun to drift away from the label as it experienced financial difficulties. In May 1966, Vee-Jay closed its offices and was declared bankrupt. Bracken returned to record retailing until his death in 1974 and Carter ran a radio station in Indiana until she died, in 1989. The important Vee-Jay catalogue is now owned and controlled by members of the Pritzker family, who are major players in the international hotel business and sponsors of the world renowned Pritzker Architect Prize.

US

No 1
Singles -
Albums -

UK

No 1
Singles **1**
Albums **14**

VERTIGO

VERTIGO

IN THE LATE '60s, when the major UK record companies began to recognise the arrival of progressive rock music, Philips chose Vertigo as the name for its underground label which they founded to rival EMI's Harvest and Decca's Deram imprints. Jazz/rock group Colosseum were among the first releases on the new label, and they were closely followed by Juicy Lucy and Black Sabbath, who kept the Vertigo flag flying in the album charts between 1970 and 1980.

After the company's name changed from Philips to Phonogram, Vertigo introduced legendary rockers Status Quo, who in 1973 began a 20-year love affair with the label after spending three years as a pop group on Pye. They were followed by Thin Lizzy, who moved over from Decca in 1975.

After a period in the doldrums as a catalogue label, Vertigo has since become re-established within the Mercury division of the Universal Music Group, and continues its rock traditions with the likes of Def Leppard (who appear on their own personal Bludgeon Rifola imprint) and Metallica (outside the US).

No 1
Singles **1**
Albums **1**

No 1
Singles **1**
Albums -

VERVE

LEADING JAZZ PROMOTER AND PRODUCER NORMAN GRANZ started Verve as a jazz label in 1957, when it boasted the world's top performers, such as Ella Fitzgerald, Charlie Parker, Dizzy Gillespie, Sarah Vaughan, Oscar Peterson and Count Basie. MGM purchased the label from Granz in 1961 for $3 million and added established jazz giants Stan Getz and Jimmy Smith before the label began to concentrate on the music of America's emerging folk rock genre.

Tim Hardin, Janis Ian, Richie Havens and Laura Nyro all appeared as Verve acts in their formative years in the mid '60s, and were followed by the intriguing pair of pop legends The Righteous Brothers and the eccentric Mothers Of Invention.

In the '70s, Verve/MGM became part of the Polygram operation, which allowed the label to wind down. However, it returned to prominence as a jazz label in the '90s in conjunction with the equally famous Impulse! label, thanks to best sellers Diana Krall and Herbie Hancock.

RCA VICTOR

VICTOR

FOUNDED IN 1922, Victor is not only one of Japan's oldest record companies but also one of its most successful. A division of the electronics giant JVC, and with links going back to America's Victory company (now owned by BMG), Victor operates in the record, music publishing and computer businesses. Huge-selling pop acts such as Southern Allstars, Ryuichi Kawamura, Kiroro, Fly, Dragon Ash, Khomi Hirose and Cocco feature on Victor's roster, alongside Japanese classical stars such as Slava.

VICTORY

FOUNDED IN CHICAGO IN THE EARLY 1990s as a hardcore punk label, Victory Records diversified into ska, rockabilly and metal under the watchful eye of founder Tony Brummel.

With a roster headed up by Snapcase, Hoods, Catch 22 and Freya, Victory sold a 25% share to MCA in 2001.

VIRGIN

RICHARD BRANSON AND NIK POWELL FIRST FORMED VIRGIN MUSIC IN 1972, after a period of selling discounted records via a magazine and from a small shop in London's East End. Twenty years later, the Virgin record label was sold to EMI for over £500 million. From one small shop, the business grew until over 30 discount record shops boasted the name Virgin.

Branson and Powell went on to acquire a 17th-century manor house in Oxfordshire and converted it into a recording studio, and this started the two young executives thinking about creating a record label. As Branson recounted in his autobiography, *Losing My Virginity*: 'If we started a Virgin record label we could offer artists somewhere to record (for which we could charge them), we could publish their songs and records (from which we could make a profit) and we had a large and growing chain of shops which could sell their records (and make the retail profit margin).'

Mike Oldfield was Virgin Records' first artist, and his album *Tubular Bells* was the label's first release and its first hit, selling over ten million copies. The roster featured the finest in early '70s alternative music, including Kevin Coyne, Hatfield And The North, Henry Cow, Tangerine Dream and Gong.

Then, in 1977 Virgin took on a band that had been dropped by two other record labels, and Branson has confirmed that this was the most significant moment in the history of his label. 'The turning point for Virgin was signing The Sex Pistols. Although the sales were not overwhelming, they put the name Virgin on the map worldwide.' Now known as the label which tamed and successfully marketed the Pistols, Virgin also embraced The Human League, Culture Club, Simple Minds, UB40 (on their own DEP International imprint) and Phil Collins. The Charisma imprint was added later, which brought Genesis and Peter Gabriel to the label.

In 1983 Virgin forged its first links with EMI to launch the famous and long-running *Now That's What I Call Music* series of compilation albums. By the late '80s, artists such as Belinda Carlisle, Paula Abdul, Madness and Stevie Winwood were also appearing on the label.

No 1
Singles **13**
Albums **8**

No 1
Singles **45**
Albums **40**

VIRGIN

As it entered the '90s, with the newly-formed subsidiary 10 launching Soul II Soul and Caron Wheeler to chart prominence, and with Circa delivering Neneh Cherry and Massive Attack, Virgin was rapidly becoming world's leading independent record company. In 1992, EMI Music acquired Virgin Music for a reported £550 million, leaving Branson free to use his Virgin name and trademark for all of his other companies, except as a record label.

Operating within the worldwide EMI Music Group, Virgin went on to forge a new empire with acts such as The Rolling Stones, Janet Jackson, Meat Loaf and George Michael (outside America). They also launched the Realworld imprint (inspired by Peter Gabriel), alongside the subsidiaries Innocent, which was home to pop acts Billie and Martine McCutcheon; Point Blank, with John Lee Hooker and Van Morrison; and the highly credible Hut division, founded by A&R executive David Boyd with award-winning acts The Verve, Gomez and The Smashing Pumpkins.

While the dance duo The Chemical Brothers have added another dimension to the Virgin label, it's a group of women, The Spice Girls – comprising Mel C, Mel G, Emma and Victoria (and not forgetting ex-member Geri, of course) – who, along with Richard Branson and Mike Oldfield, were for five years the people most publicly associated with the name Virgin.

The new millennium brought a closer merging of the Virgin and EMI operations and management, although the individual labels retained their own identities and artist rosters, with Innocent home to Blue and Atomic Kitten, Source delivering Turin Brakes and Virgin having success with The Chemical Brothers, Massive Attack and Aaliyah.

No 1
Singles **1**
Albums -

No 1
Singles -
Albums -

VP

APPROPRIATELY LOCATED IN NEW YORK'S JAMAICA TOWNSHIP, VP Records is acknowledged as one of the world's premiere independent reggae labels.

Vincent and Patricia (VP) Chin first entered the jukebox business in Kingston, Jamaica, in the 1950s and in 1958 opened a retail store and landmark recording studio, which was frequented by the likes of Bob Marley and Peter Tosh.

After moving to America in the 1970s, the Chins established the retail store VP Records in Jamaica, in New York's Queens district, in 1979. VP Records grew to encompass retail, concert promotion and a record label boasting the likes of Shabba Ranks, Beenie Man and Gregory Isaacs.

Vincent Chin, who died in 2003 aged 65, had handed over the running of VP Records to his sons and grandson and in 2002 the label formed a joint venture with Atlantic Records which launched the careers of Sean Paul and Wayne Wonder.

No 1
Singles -
Albums -

No 1
Singles **2**
Albums **4**

V2

IN 1996, FOUR YEARS AFTER HE SOLD HIS VIRGIN MUSIC EMPIRE TO EMI, Richard Branson embarked on a new music venture, establishing the V2 record company as part of his Virgin Group. The V2 label is in fact the only company in Branson's Virgin empire which doesn't carry the Virgin logo, reflecting the conditions of EMI Music's acquisition of the Virgin music operations in 1992.

V2 opened with operations around the world, which was something Branson has gone on record as saying that he learned from his early Virgin days. 'When setting up V2, the thing I remembered from Virgin was to be truly international, which is why V2 was in every country from day one.' Following the initial success of The Stereophonics, V2 linked with the impressive dance label Junior Boy's Own (home to dance favourites Underworld and Farley And Heller), acquired the rap label Gee Street and absorbed Big Cat Records into the set-up in 1999.

V2 boasted a growing roster, featuring The Jungle Brothers, Gravediggaz, Kirsty MacColl and Mercury Rev. The label has also enjoyed international success with its V2 affiliates, with acts such as Passi and Alex Gopher from France, Postmen from Holland, DJ Ian Pooley from Germany, and the highly-successful dance star Moby in America. In recent times, V2 has reduced its international presence and focussed on domestic A&R, delivering new act Liberty X, before a cash injection of £128 million from merchant bankers revived the label, which most recently added Tom Jones and Paul Weller to the roster.

VALIANT – see Warner Bros

VELVEL – see Koch

VOCALION – see CBS/Warner Bros

VOGUE – see Coral

VOLCANO – see Zomba

VOLT – see Stax

RECORDS

WARNER BROS

THE HOME OF SUPERSTAR ACTS SUCH AS MADONNA, REM, Rod Stewart and Eric Clapton, Warner Bros Records has more than made up for the failure of the original record company, which was launched by the famous film studio over 70 years ago.

Already established as a major film company in the '20s by Harry, Sam and Jack Warner, the original Warner Feature Film Company had first experimented with sound recording in 1925 by developing sound motion pictures (which weren't talkies but featured music) in association with the company Western Electric. The very first sound motion picture was *Don Juan*, and two years later a film titled *The Jazz Singer* appeared, featuring Al Jolson singing and talking, which made the studio a household name and fuelled Warner Bros' interest in sound and music.

The studio bought Brunswick Records in 1930, but despite boasting best-selling artist Bing Crosby as its major star the business failed, falling victim to the Depression, which saw record sales plummet from a 1927 figure of 104 million discs to just six million in 1932. Harry Warner decided to quit the record business, and sold the Brunswick operation, including its subsidiary Vocalion, to ARC (the American Record Company) in 1932.

It was nearly 30 years before Jack Warner took steps towards re-establishing his film company in the recorded music business. When his efforts to acquire Imperial failed, he decided to launch Warner Bros Records in 1958, with a start-up budget of $3 million.

In September of the same year, the first twelve Warner Bros Records were issued, including releases by Connie Stevens and Henry Mancini. However, the label's first hit came from one of the television shows made in the Warner studio. *77 Sunset Strip* star Ed Byrnes charted in 1958, as his character Kookie Byrnes, with 'Kookie Kookie Lend Me Your Comb'. Comedians Bob Newhart and Alan Sherman actually brought the label four of its first five American Number One albums, and they were joined on the label by Peter Paul And Mary and Warner Bros' first chart-topping singles act, The Everly Brothers. It was the success of

WARNER BROS

Newhart and Don and Phil Everly that actually kept the label afloat, after the original $3 million had been lost and over 100 employees had been laid off within the first two years.

The next significant move in the development of Warner Bros Records came when Jack Warner decided that he wanted to sign singer Frank Sinatra to a four-film deal with Warner Bros Films. Sinatra's own Reprise label was in debt, and the singer wanted to move on. Warner Bros left Sinatra with a third of his label and gave him $2 million and a four-picture deal for the remaining two-thirds share of Reprise Records, which featured Sinatra, Trini Lopez and Dean Martin.

Bill Cosby maintained the label's success rate in marketing comedians on record, and in 1965 Warner Bros acquired its first two independent labels, Valiant and Autumn, whose rosters included The Association and Harpers Bizarre respectively.

With the emergence of rock, the label signed The Grateful Dead in 1966. However, within a year, Warner Bros Records – along with the film and TV companies and the studios – were acquired by Seven Arts, who changed the name of the parent company to Warner Bros-Seven Arts. In 1969, the two-year-old company was bought by the Kinney Corporation, who also added Atlantic Records to the fold. Despite the changes in ownership, Warner Bros Records continued to grow, adding to the label James Taylor, Van Morrison, America, Alice Cooper, The Doobie Brothers and Fleetwood Mac, who switched from Reprise, as well as UK signings The Faces, featuring Rod Stewart,

The '80s saw more success for Warner Bros thanks to Van Halen, George Benson and Paul Simon. At the same time, the subsidiary label Sire discovered a young lady calling herself Madonna, and Prince also emerged from Minneapolis to complete the signing of two of pop music's most controversial artists to the same company.

In 1988 Warner Bros Records secured REM, whose singer Michael Stipe is reported to have said that the reason why his group signed to Warner Bros was 'Bugs Bunny'. In the '90s, Warner maintained its position as one of the world's

No 1
Singles **35**
Albums **30**

No 1
Singles **10**
Albums **21**

WARNER BROS

major record labels thanks to kd lang and Red Hot Chili Peppers, as well as successful soundtracks from the *Batman* movies, *Evita* and *Space Jam*. At the same time, Maverick – the joint-venture label owned with Madonna – delivered record breaking Canadian singer Alanis Morissette, alongside the label's own hit signings Faith Hill and The Goo Goo Dolls. After the millennium, one of the world's leading new bands emerged on Warner Bros when Linkin Park notched up global sales of over 15 million with their first two albums, alongside renewed success for label veterans Red Hot Chili Peppers.

WARNER MUSIC

WARNER MUSIC GROUP, A DIVISION OF AOL TIME WARNER, is the only major American-owned music operation. The company consists of Atlantic Records, Elektra Entertainment, Warner Bros Records, Warner Music International (which operates in 70 countries outside the US) and Warner Chappell music publishing.

The company's music operations began in the '30s with a short-lived venture by the Warner Brothers film company, who re-entered music in 1958 with Warner Bros Records. Reprise was added a few years later.

Following the acquisition of Warner Brothers by Seven Arts in 1967, the new Warner-Seven Arts company proceeded to buy Atlantic Records. In 1969, the American corporation Kinney National – a combination of New York's Kinney Parking Company and National Cleaning Company, which were both formed in 1932 and which merged in 1966 – bought Warner-Seven Arts. The Elektra/Asylum label was added a year later to create the US-based WEA group of labels and the WEA International company, later to be re-named Warner Music International.

In 1971 Kinney National was renamed Warner Communications Inc, and in 1983 WCI launched a plan to merge its music operation with Polygram's records division to create the world's biggest music company. In 1984, America's Federal Trade Commission finally refused to sanction the proposed merger. Six years later, however, WCI Chairman Steve Ross successfully completed a merger with Time Inc to form Time Warner, the world's largest media and entertainment corporation.

In 2000 the American Internet company AOL (America Online) announced their acquisition of Time Warner and the creation of one of the world's leading conglomerates. This news was followed by official confirmation of a planned merger of the Warner Music Group with EMI Music, which was abandoned in the face of objections from the European commission. Since then, the company has forged links with US labels Word, Curb and Giant and acquired international companies such as London, Mushroom UK, Peerless and Milan.

WARP

ROB MITCHELL AND STEVE BECKETT grew into their own Warp label from the FON record store that they ran in Sheffield. The shop was home to members of the local dance fraternity, who convinced the duo to issue Forgemaster's 'Track With No Name'. The success of this experimental release resulted in the inauguration of Warp in 1989, and within a year Tricky Disco and LSO had provided the label's first Top 40 hits. The start of the highly regarded Artificial Intelligence series began in 1992, at the same time that Aphex Twin signed to the label.

Plaid, Autechre, Red Snapper and ex-Cabaret Voltaire man Richard Kirk have all signed to Warp, which has been dubbed 'the temple of the weird'. The techno/modern elec-tronica label celebrated ten years in the business in 1999 with a triple-CD release entitled *Warps 10 + 1, 2 And 3*.

No 1
Singles -
Albums -

No 1
Singles **10**
Albums **5**

WEA

THE INITIALS WEA STAND FOR THE WARNER BROS, ELEKTRA AND ATLANTIC LABELS within the Warner Music Group. The label first came into existence in 1970, with the creation of the company's first American distribution arm and its international operation. Since then WEA has been established in the UK – and in other Warner Music International territories – as a leading label identity, and the company which handles US repertoire from the Warner Music Group's labels.

Deals with the imprints Real and Korova brought WEA The Pretenders and Echo And The Bunnymen, until the WEA label first appeared in the British charts in 1980 with Dollar and, a year later, Modern Romance. British talent such as Howard Jones, Aztec Camera, Matt Bianco and Tanita Tikaram surfaced on WEA during the '80s, alongside the million-selling American superstars coming from Warner Bros, Elektra and Atlantic.

While Enya, Elaine Paige, Mike Oldfield, Mark Morrison and Cher all tasted success as direct WEA UK signings, the company's subsidiary labels Blanco Y Negro (home to Everything But The Girl, Eddi Reader and Catatonia) and Eternal (with Eiffel 65 and Black Legend) also secured important chart success for WEA, alongside emerging acts Shola Ama and Cleopatra. Linked with London Records in the UK since 2001, WEA delivered H & Claire alongside The Streets via its link with 679 Recordings.

No 1
Singles **1**
Albums **2**

No 1
Singles **1**
Albums **1**

WIND-UP

FORMER CD WHOLESALER and record retailer Alan Meltzer and partner Steven Lerner founded Wind-Up in 1997 on the back of Meltzer's $5 million investment and a band found by Meltzer's wife Diana.

Mrs Meltzer heard a home-produced tape of a rock band from Florida and within a week Creed had switched from local label Blue Collar to become New York-based Wind-Up's first and only act.

Benefiting from the skills of partner Steven Lerner, former head of Castle Communications US, Wind-Up saw Creed's album sales run into millions and establish the five-year-old label as a major player, distributed in the US by BMG and by Sony internationally. The group Evanescence brought more success to the label which was among the first to focus on Internet marketing involving retail websites.

WINDHAM HILL

WINDHAM HILL

OVER THE YEARS, WINDHAM HILL has grown to become one of the world's leading new age/adult instrumental music labels, boasting among its roster of artists the hit makers Barry White, Peabo Bryson and Jeffrey Osborne.

Husband-and-wife team Anne Robinson and William Ackerman began the label in California in 1976 and watched it grow with the signing of artists such as Jim Brickman, Ray Lynch and The Modern Mandolin Quartet, as well as labels High Street and Dancing Cat.

In 1992, BMG acquired 50% of Windham Hill and bought the outstanding half in 1995. Since then, new artists such as Michael Hedges and Liz Story have emerged, to appear alongside veteran Brickman, Janis Ian and George Winston.

WORD ENTERTAINMENT

ONE OF THE WORLD'S LEADING CHRISTIAN MUSIC COMPANIES, WORD WAS SET UP IN WACO, TEXAS, IN 1952 but moved to Nashville – the heart of America's southern music business – in 1993 after it was purchased by Gaylord Entertainment for $110 million.

The company has two record labels, Word and Myrr, which feature artists such as Amy Grant (who had five UK Top 50 hits in the early '90s), Kirk Franklin, Point Of Grace and hit makers Sixpence None The Richer. Combined, they account for over 30% of America's profitable Christian record market. In 2001, Warner Music Group bought Word from Gaylord and acquired leading Christian music artists Jaci Velasquez and Sandi Patty, plus access to the Integrity and Big Idea labels.

WALT DISNEY – see Hollywood

WIIJA – see Beggars Banquet Group

WILDSTAR – see Telstar

XL

AN EARLY DANCE VENTURE LABEL called City Beat
Records, in the words of owners Beggars Banquet,
'spawned' XL Recordings in 1989 as a 'house' label under
the direction of Richard Russell.

The label's first hits came in 1991 with SL2 and Liquid,
but it was chart toppers Prodigy (whose seven-million-selling
The Fat Of The Land album topped the charts in 27 different
countries) who brought a new sort of pop presence to the
Beggars stable.

XL's development continued in the late 1990s with
Basement Jaxx and Badly Drawn Boy, followed by the label's
latest hit with US indie band The White Stripes.

ZOMBA

ACKNOWLEDGED AS THE WORLD'S PREMIER INDEPENDENT MUSIC COMPANY, Zomba was founded in the UK by South African Clive Calder, who now runs his empire from America and boasts the chart-topping Jive label among his company's prime assets. The first Zomba company was a book publishing venture, which started life in 1977, but after buying a studio and managing record producers Calder moved into the record business in 1981. The first hit record was released on Jive in the same year, by Tight Fit.

Alongside the UK-based label Jive, Zomba has grown to include operations in Australia, Canada, France, Holland, Germany and Singapore. The company also includes the American Christian music companies Brentwood and Benson; record labels Silvertone, Verity, Volcano and Music For Nations; the long-established UK distribution business Pinnacle, which was added in 1996; and Germany's Rough Trade. The Battery Studios management company and significant music-publishing interests complete the Zomba empire, which in 1996 sold a 20% minority interest in its record division to BMG Entertainment, long-time distributors of Zomba repertoire in America. Calder – who left EMI's South African office in 1970 to form his first company, CCP Records, and moved to the UK in 1974 – has created a highly-successful business, with sales in 1999 exceeding the $1 billion mark.

The man who describes himself as the founder of Zomba, but refuses to be drawn on the situation of the company's ownership, consistently denies rumours of a sell-out. 'Zomba is not for sale. I believe that music-driven companies should not be publicly owned because it is so difficult to maintain continuity of earnings.' However, Calder had a change of heart in 2002 when he decided to sell his company to the German media company Bertelsmann, owners of BMG Music, for $2.7 billion.

No 1
Singles **1**
Albums **3**

No 1
Singles **2**
Albums **3**

ZTT

PRODUCER TREVOR HORN had been half of the duo Buggles, who topped the chart with 'Video Killed The Radio Star', before he created ZTT Records with his wife, Jill Sinclair, in 1982. When forming ZTT, he adopted what he later called a romanticised but naïve view. 'Having our own record company would allow me to help on projects, albums or recording sessions, even if I wasn't producing.'

Financed by Island Records, ZTT (an abbreviation of the phrase Zang Tumb Tuum, used in an Italian war poem to describe the noise of a machine gun) first launched the act Art Of Noise before hitting the big time with Frankie Goes To Hollywood, with their controversial lyrics and eye-catching artwork. Together with Propaganda, Art Of Noise and Frankie ensured that, in 1983, ZTT had a record in the UK Top 75 singles chart in every week of the year.

After fleeting success with Grace Jones, the label became independent in 1986, acquiring the right to buy the now-defunct Stiff Records label before entering into a joint venture agreement with Warner Music UK. Hits from Shades Of Rhythm and 808 State paved the way for the success of Seal (produced by Horn), who emerged as the next big ZTT act before he switched to the US-based label Warner Bros.

ZTT split from Warner in 1998 and regained its independent status in the UK, with a roster which featured the reformed Art Of Noise, Leilani and Fragile. The label went on to forge links with Universal Records in America to obtain distribution and marketing support.